THE HUSBAND HANDBOOK

WILLIAM E. RABIOR
DAVID WACHOWIAK

Liguori

ONE LIGUORI DRIVE
LIGUORI MO 63057-9999

Imprimi Potest:
Thomas D. Picton, C.Ss.R.
Provincial, Denver Province
The Redemptorists

Published by Liguori Publications
Liguori, Missouri
To order, call 800-325-9521 or visit www.liguori.org

Library of Congress Cataloging-in-Publication Data

Rabior, William E.
    The husband handbook / William E. Rabior and
David Wachowiak.
        p. cm.
    ISBN 978-0-7648-1745-8
    1. Husbands—Religious life. 2. Marriage—Religious
aspects—Christianity. I. Wachowiak, David. II. Title.
BV4528.3.R33 2008
248.8'425—dc22   2008020205

Scripture quotations are from *New Revised Standard Version Bible*, copy-
right © 1989 National Council of the Churches of Christ in the United
States of America. Used by permission. All rights reserved.

Liguori Publications, a nonprofit corporation, is an apostolate of the
Redemptorists. To learn more about the Redemptorists, visit *Redemptor-
ists.com*.

Printed in the United States of America
11 10 09 08   4 3 2 1
First edition

We dedicate this book with love to our wives:
Susan Wachowiak and Susan Charters Rabior,
to whom we ourselves are dedicated.

We also wish to thank our editor, Alicia von Stamwitz, for her help, encouragement, and invaluable insights.

BLESSING PRAYER

God of all good gifts, thank you for the gift of married life and love and for the special role of husband in marriage.

Look with kindness and compassion upon husbands of all ages and places, and especially those who are guided by your Holy Spirit to this book.

May your Spirit use this book to touch them and minister to them.

May this book help them identify their own needs and the needs of their wife, and show them how to meet those needs in healthy ways that lead to happy outcomes.

Grace their marriage with peace and healing. May they replace barriers with bridges, and learn how to transform their tribulations and trials into triumphs for themselves and their spouse.

By giving may they receive all that their hearts desire, and by loving may they be loved lavishly in return.

May their families bring them joy, their friends, comfort, and their faith, strength. May they and their wife always find a home in each other's heart.

Gracious God, with all our hearts we bless them, and we ask you to bless them, too. Amen.

CONTENTS

INTRODUCTION

Every marriage—yours, ours, everyone's—is a work in progress. Each partner in any marriage could legitimately say to the other, "Please be patient with me, God isn't finished with me yet. And I'm not finished with me either."

Every marriage is evolving and in an unfinished state. We who are married know that our marriage could always be something more than it already is—a little better, a little richer, a little more fulfilling. Most of us who are married want it to be more, not less. And the truth is a marriage can go from bad to good, good to great, great to even greater, if we only commit ourselves to doing the kind of marital work that will propel it forward.

And that is why we wrote this handbook.

We wrote it not because we are perfect husbands in perfect marriages or because we want the husbands who read it to be perfect. We just wanted to share with other husbands (and wives) the fruits of our marital successes and failures, our insights, the outcomes from our trials and triumphs, with the hope that in some ways they might all be of some help to the reader.

We believe that the role of husband is a special one in marriage. He is called on to be leader, protector, nurturer, guide, and much more—not in competition with his wife, but in collaboration with her. If husbands become stronger, marriages will become stronger and so will families, and that is something we all want.

We are each very proud to be a husband. It was a role we deliberately chose years ago, and one that has been a source of almost indescribable blessings for us.

This book proved to be both a window and a mirror on our own marriages. It caused us to look carefully and closely at our marriages and to see what was reflected as we wrote. It has been an important learning experience for each of us. We both feel that we are better husbands for having written this handbook, and we hope you will be, too, for having read it.

If what we wrote can help heal a hurt in your marriage, replace a barrier with a bridge, pump in some fresh air, and draw you closer to each other, then we will be enormously pleased, and this book will have been a success and well worth all the effort it took to write it. May you and your wife become all that you can be, individually and together.

We wish you the best of blessings.

William E. Rabior
David Wachowiak

CHAPTER ONE

MAKE YOUR MARRIAGE YOUR HOBBY

"Gosh darn it! When are you going to love me as much as you love the Yankees?" (Wife to husband, overheard on a New York subway)

One day Todd decided to take up golf. He is a true perfectionist who puts everything he has into whatever task he strives to master. Unfortunately, no one ever told Todd that even the very best professional golfers have bad days on the golf course and experience many frustrating rounds. He has found out that golf is an easy game to play, but a hard game to play well.

Nonetheless, Todd gives golf his all. He buys books, videos, subscribes to golfing magazines, and has purchased clubs that cost nearly the same amount as a hefty down payment on a new car.

Going to the links to play and the driving range to practice are now virtually everyday occurrences for Todd. He has been transformed into a true fanatic about his new hobby of golf. To those who are willing to listen he talks about every aspect of golf, from the best places to play to the wide variety of golf paraphernalia available (for those who have everything, there are always ball warmers).

Todd is totally committed to the sport, but he has always

remained a responsible golfer. His equipment purchases and golfing excursions are carefully budgeted and have not become a burden on his family. He would never miss an important family event because of the game. He has kept his golfing hobby in perspective and his priorities straight. His marriage and family come first, and his wife knows that, but nevertheless the hobby has energized him and brought excitement to his life. "I love the game," he says, almost gleefully. "I've had lots of hobbies throughout my life, but nothing that has brought me as much pleasure as golf—even if I never get a hole in one or turn pro."

Albert has experienced the same kind of exuberance. After he retired, he joined a local archaeology club. Under the direction of a trained archaeologist, he joins six other retirees twice a week to take part in a dig where ancient artifacts are found. What does he say about his new hobby? "It makes history come alive, and me, too." He adds with a broad smile, "When I'm at the site of the dig, shoveling dirt, and finding arrowheads, I feel like I'm a kid again, although my aching back later reminds me otherwise. But for me, this is a hobby made in heaven. I love doing it."

A husband with a hobby he genuinely loves gives his time, money, energy, and interest to it. He is fully committed to it, and it shows. His heart is in his hobby. If you are a husband who relates to this kind of hobby talk, we would simply ask: Doesn't your marriage deserve equal time? Can you make your marriage your hobby? Make your marriage every bit the priority that your favorite hobby or pastime has in your life, and then extend yourself and go for even more.

What does making our marriage our hobby mean? It means that we give as much of ourselves to our relationship with our wife as we do to the favorite hobby to which we are drawn. Here are a few suggestions to better clarify this notion.

1. There's hobby language and marriage language. Both have a purpose, and both need to be learned. When Todd took up golfing, he had to learn words such as birdie, eagle, mulligan, and links. Each hobby has its own special and unique language. Marriage does, too. The language of marriage, which is fundamentally the language of love, can be as simple or complex as you are. Creativity is important here and can greatly enrich a marital relationship. For example, why limit yourself to pet names such as "Honey" or "Sweetheart?" How about trying a Romance language like French or Spanish: "Je t'adore" ("I adore you"), Je t'aime, ma cherie ("I love you, my darling"), or "Te amo" ("I love you")?

   And what about the message given by body language? In marriage—like every other area of life—how you present yourself matters. Walking around the house in various stages of dress with stubble on your face may seem manly, but for most wives it's a turn-off, even though young Hollywood leading men seem to always have a five o'clock shadow.

   If you really want to touch your wife's heart, try using song language or the language of poetry. Have you ever sung to your wife? Try it sometime and see what happens. And what about poetry? A husband and wife were celebrating their twenty-fifth wedding anniversary with a special dinner. He made a toast to her in which he said among other things that the light dimmed when she wasn't with him. She melted.

2. Make a commitment of time to your marriage. Husbands with a hobby they really like will give it unlimited time. A marriage relationship deserves the same. Nurturing and cultivating a deep relationship with your wife are byproducts of spending quality time with her. Ted had the right idea. "My hobby is fishing. If I am going on a fishing trip with my buddies, I tell my wife she is entitled to equal time. I let her choose a spot

where we can have a long weekend together, and we make it happen. It's only fair." Regular time spent with your wife provides a setting where your marriage is strengthened. You can learn to talk to each other about the little, everyday things that go with married life, in addition to the big, important, life-changing things when they arise. You can talk about anything and everything, because spending time together has made you friends, not strangers.

3. Put zeal and zest into your marriage, like you would with your favorite hobby. Gary is a huge fan of the Pittsburgh Steelers, and he doesn't hesitate to let the whole world know it. He not only watches his team play on television and at stadiums all over the country, he wears their logo on a variety of clothing. He practically gets lost in his hobby.

   You don't have to follow the Steelers like Gary does, but how about becoming your wife's biggest fan and showing that by what you say and do? Do you have a picture of her in your wallet? At your workplace or desk? Do you remember your wedding anniversary and other important dates like her birthday without being reminded? How many years have you been married? (That one you should know instantaneously.) Do you listen as she talks about her hopes and wishes, so that you know what is important to her? Finding things that you like in common and can do together are important aspects of a marriage relationship. Suggesting that the two of you go see that "chick flick" she's talked about for days or letting her pick out the next movie rental and watching it without grumbling can become sensitive and much-appreciated gifts for her. Investing the same kind of energy in your marriage that you do with your favorite hobby can re-energize, re-invigorate, and renew your marriage. Give it a try.

4. And as long as we are on the subject: Find a hobby that appeals to both you and your wife—something the two of you can do together. For many years Fred's favorite hobby was stamp collecting, a relatively solitary pursuit that did not interest his wife, Elaine. Then, one day some friends suggested the two of them try square dancing. With some trepidation Fred and Elaine went to their first square dance, and to their amazement they really liked it. So much, in fact, that they joined a square dance club and dance several times a week. They now have a hobby they can share in common, one that is good for each of them and very good for their marriage.

Make your marriage your hobby, and give it your all. But don't be content to merely give it as much as your favorite hobby. Stretch yourself—give it even more. The payoff to you and your wife is likely to be greater than you might imagine.

Things to Think About

1. Do you devote as much time to your marriage as you do to your favorite pastime?
2. Is there a hobby you and you wife could do together? If there isn't, could you find one?

CHAPTER TWO

PRACTICING THE ART OF MARITAL MAINTENANCE

"I love my kids, I love my wife. But my '68 Mustang is the real love of my life." (Overheard at a church picnic)

Whoever composed that little ditty had his priorities pretty lopsided. Loving things more than people is a sure-fire recipe for relationship disaster. But it does underscore the sometimes irrational exuberance men have for machines—cars, trucks, motorcycles, and a host of others. Many guys view the internal combustion engine as the crowning achievement and zenith of all human inventions.

Millions of husbands everywhere on this planet enjoy tinkering with engines of every kind and purpose. And they understand that maintenance is the key to good performance and reliability. It's consistent maintenance that keeps anything with a motor running.

Now, we know full well that there is nothing mechanical about marriage, and using the metaphor of a vehicle to describe marriage is bound to limp a little, but the concept of marital maintenance is not so far-fetched. "It makes perfect sense to me," said one husband. "In lots of respects, marriage is just like an automobile. If you keep it fueled with love, oil it with care, consideration, and some occasional pampering of your spouse, and now and then put in an additive like some extra special romance, it will run forever." He laughed. "I should know. It's what I do, and my marriage has been running smoothly for almost thirty-five years."

Marital maintenance simply means a husband, wife—preferably both—develop a sense of what is and what is not working well in a marriage. What needs attention? What needs fixing? What should be discarded and relegated to the junk heap? What should not be tinkered with, because it is working smoothly and gives the relationship power, strength, and resilience? What needs just a touch of fine-tuning to make it run even better?

What follows is a kind of marital checklist for maintaining a smooth-running marriage. It doesn't cover every aspect of marriage, but it touches many of the important areas. As you read it, be honest with yourself. It will give you a sense of what is happening in your marriage—where you are strong and areas that might be tweaked for a better, happier, and more harmonious relationship between yourself and your spouse.

How well do you really know your wife? For example, do you know her favorite food, song, color, best friend, or flower? (There is an old joke about a marriage counselor who asked a husband what his wife's favorite flower was. The husband didn't hesitate for an instant: "Pillsbury, All-Purpose," he responded proudly.)

1. When was the last time you hugged your wife? Kissed her?
2. When was the last time you told her she looks beautiful?
3. When did you last tell her you love her?
4. When was the last time you two made love?
5. When was the last time you sent her a love letter or note?
6. How long has it been since you had a romantic dinner alone with your wife?

7. Wives love to be helped around the house. When was the last time you helped put the kids to bed, did the dishes or the laundry, or vacuumed without being asked?
8. Did you remember your last wedding anniversary with flowers, a gift, or a card?
9. Have you ever planned a surprise weekend where the two of you got away alone?
10. When was the last time you let her sleep in?
11. When did you last phone your spouse during the day to say you were thinking about her?
12. When was the last time you bought her an unexpected little gift like perfume, a piece of jewelry, or an item of clothing she has really wanted?
13. When was the last time you felt you really communicated your needs to your wife?
14. When was the last time she communicated her needs to you, and you really tried to understand what she was telling you?
15. When did you last compliment her?
16. When was the last time you two had a fight that was win-win?
17. When did you last feel that the two of you were truly growing and changing together, and you felt confident about your future together?
18. When was the last time you felt that both of you had a really satisfying sexual experience together?
19. When was the last time you listened deeply to your wife and accepted her feelings just the way she expressed them without providing your own interpretation?
20. When did you last apologize to your wife or tell her you were sorry about something?
21. If she is overstressed right now, do you know what the main stressors are?

22. What are some of her special dreams or deepest longings?
23. When was the last time the two of you prayed together?
24. Are you and your wife soul mates?
25. Do you think of your wife as your best friend? Why or why not?
26. The last time you were angry at your wife, how did you handle your anger?
27. When was the last time you discussed your finances with her?
28. Are you presently engaged in any behaviors that might be dangerous to the well-being of your marriage?
29. Are passion and fire still present in your marriage?
30. Are you respectful of your wife?
31. Do you ever physically, verbally, or mentally abuse her?
32. Have you recently told her how glad you are that you married her?
33. What is the most healing thing you could do for your wife?
34. At the present time, do you think you and your wife would benefit from marriage counseling? If so, why?
35. Do you have secrets you are keeping from her?
36. What is the strongest aspect of your marriage?
37. What could be improved upon?
38. What never fails to give your marriage a boost?
39. If you have a good marriage, what would it take to get you and your wife to a great marriage?

We asked several husbands what they thought of this notion of practicing marriage maintenance. Every one of them felt it made sense. "My wife and I sit down once a year, around the time of our wedding anniversary," one husband told us, "and we review the year together. We look at how we are doing as a couple, and then we renew our marriage vows. For us, this is one of the high points of the entire year." "There is never any harm in checking to see if everything is running well," said another. "Sometimes, a little preventive maintenance can stop a whole lot of bigger problems from happening."

The heart of marital maintenance is really about making more love for your marriage. No matter how it is done, if it can prevent a problem from developing, solve or resolve a conflict, or nip a potential crisis in the bud, it is worth all the time and effort you put into it, and you and your wife are the big winners.

Things to Think About

1. Does this idea of marital maintenance make sense to you?
2. If so, do you already practice it?
3. If not, why not?

CHAPTER THREE

MONEY MATTERS

Husband to wife: "I want to retire." "Retire!" "But do we have enough money?" "Sure, we have plenty of money to last us the rest of our lives...as long as we don't buy anything."

here is a very old story about four blind men who were asked to describe an elephant by touch alone. One felt the elephant's tail and described him as long and thin. One felt a leg and said the animal was thick and stocky. A third felt a tusk and said this beast was clearly made of horn. The last blind man stroked an ear and said the animal was silky and smooth. From this simple experiment came four very different interpretations of the same reality.

Many husbands and wives approach their finances in the same way. They are dealing with the same reality, but they may have different, and often conflicting, interpretations and opinions as to how those finances should be managed. One spouse may be a spender, the other a saver. The spouse who makes the most money may feel she or he should also have the most to say about how it is spent. One spouse may be impulsive, the other very cautious and deliberate.

Small wonder that marriage therapists almost universally agree that the number one presenting problem couples bring to their offices is conflict over finances—fights over money that somehow never seem to get resolved and over time take a toll on the marriage relationship. The truth is that money really does matter, and although it should not, in many marriages money issues take center stage.

We asked several husbands to comment on the role that money management plays in their marriage. Here is a sampling of what they said.

Reed: "Sure, my wife and I fight over finances. We've been married eight years, and we have yet to create a budget. As a result, usually there is too much month and not enough money, and we end up so frustrated that we take it out on each other. Individually, we both know how to handle our money, but doing it together is a whole other story."

Steve: "I have to admit that we are both somewhat reckless when it comes to our credit cards. Each of us tends to charge too much, then we end up with a large balance and can usually only afford to pay the minimum payment. Having a lot of credit card debt hanging over us is a big source of our financial stress."

Adam: "My wife and I battled for years over money issues. Then, a surprising thing happened. As part of a marriage enrichment program, our parish offered a communications workshop for couples, and we took it. It helped us develop some new communications skills that we agreed to try. What's funny is that once we started communicating better, our fighting over money got less and less, until eventually it became almost nonexistent.

From hindsight, it became obvious to us that our main problem wasn't the money. Our problem was that we just didn't know how to talk to each other about it."

Marriage researchers have conducted studies for years on the impact of finances on marriages. Their conclusion—it's huge. In survey after survey couples have identified money problems as the one issue they argue about the most. It is also frequently named as the principal factor for ending a marriage. Clearly, in marriage it is a force to be reckoned with.

If you and your wife have your own money matters under control, our congratulations and well done! You should make it a point to congratulate each other. Successfully managing money in a marriage is no small achievement.

However, if money matters are problematic for the two of you, and if you are looking for a few suggestions that might help you and your spouse address your finances in a healthier, and perhaps less contentious way, consider the following ideas.

First, we all might learn a lesson from Adam's experience and look at the ways we communicate with our wife about money matters. Surveys show that as many as 70 percent of couples discuss money every week, but marital woes over this issue still doggedly persist.

The problem seems to be in the ways communication does or does not take place. Instead of really talking about their financial concerns, couples most likely are talking *at* each other so that productive dialogue does not occur and nothing gets resolved.

"My wife and I never seem to get anywhere when we talk about money," one husband told us. "It's too emotional an issue, and as soon as the subject turns to money, one or both of us react negatively, and the whole thing becomes an exercise in futility."

Sometimes striving to really listen to what the other is saying, and making a commitment to work together as a team to address money matters de-escalates some of the emotional content, such as being angry at or resentful of your spouse. As a result, things become more productive and more manageable.

Ask yourself this question: Is this financial issue worth fighting or bickering about, or is there something we can instead do together to resolve it? Try to look at the issue more strategically in a problem-solving way, instead of just emotionally, and see what happens.

Second, hammer out a budget with your wife, even a relatively simple one, and then stick to it. Many of us engage in impulse buying and spending, which can turn family finances into a train wreck, or we spend our money without seeing the whole financial picture and then hope for the best.

A budget provides a better sense of where our money is going or should be going. It also matches our spending with our priorities. By helping to keep spending in check, it creates more financial stability, which directly affects the overall stability of the marriage in general.

Third, work together to reduce any debt that you may have. It's a well-known fact that many Americans are drowning in a sea of debt. Anything you and your wife can do to chip away at what you owe is definitely in your best interest as a couple. By steadily working at reducing your debt and making it more manageable, you are paving the way for a better and safer financial future together.

Fourth, be honest about your own personal finances and the overall financial situation of your marriage. Concealing or withholding information, hiding things, or not being candid when it comes to money matters usually leads to far more problems than solutions.

Things that are hidden have a way of being discovered eventually anyway, and the fabric of the marriage may then be torn and irreparably damaged by the dishonesty and deception. Don't play games with each other when it comes to your finances. Tell the truth, and let it set you both free.

Fifth, stay on top of your money matters. At least once a year, but preferably even more often than that, take a look at where you and your wife stand financially. Have an annual financial meeting at which you examine your current debts and assets, and look at such important areas as insurance, beneficiaries on your various accounts, and your overall goals.

Organize your important documents so that they are easily accessible if there is a crisis, and especially if you or your spouse become ill or die. Many wives complain that they lack financial information. Is this true of your wife, and if it is, could you provide her with what she needs to know should you not be there?

Finally, if you need help, get it. Every community has credit counselors, financial planners, and professional advisers who can be of assistance, if only you ask for it. More and more churches are offering classes on financial matters. There are also local agencies that will help low- or middle-income families learn how to prepare a budget and balance a checkbook. If you are a senior citizen, many senior centers offer free assistance with tax preparation and other financial matters. Today there is also much financial advice available on the Internet as well. If you feel overwhelmed by your financial situation and need guidance, look for it, ask for it, and then accept it. It may help provide a light that leads you out of financial darkness into the light.

Remember: one of the most important goals of marriage is to learn how to function reasonably well as a team. Spouses who function as lone rangers, whether it be in the financial sector of marriage or any other area, are setting themselves and their marriage up for serious problems. Whatever you do and however you decide to do it, do it *together*. Address your money matters with shared communication and a collaborative approach, and see how much easier their resolution becomes.

Things to Think About

1. Have you and your wife talked recently about the financial state of your marriage?
2. If you haven't, could you do so soon?
3. Do the two of you work together as a team when it comes to the money matters in your marriage? If not, why not?

CHAPTER FOUR

SPIRITUALITY

Son to father: "Hey, Dad, I guess Mom's Bible must be more interesting than yours." Father: "Why do you say that?" Son: "Because she reads it more than you read yours."

"Do what you can do, and pray for what you cannot yet do." (Old spiritual maxim)

The word *spirituality* has become a catchall expression for various aspects of religion—any religion—just as Kleenex is used for tissue or Xerox for a photocopy. In fact, even though most people think of *spirituality* and *religion* as equal in meaning, they are different.

Religion is made up of creeds, dogmas, rituals, and generally a communal expression of beliefs. *Spirituality* refers more to the fire that burns within us—what moves us, motivates us, stirs us, and drives our life. It is our primary energy center where we encounter the transcendent or divine dimension of our existence. Hopefully, our spirituality enriches our religious faith and our religious faith enriches our spirituality, so that each benefits from the other and nurtures the other.

Our spirituality is uniquely our own, formed by many factors, including the people we have encountered, life experiences, and even the historical times in which we live. We are not always able to express our spirituality in words, so some turn to the arts—painting, poetry, music. Others savor a beautiful sunset, a soaring eagle, or the cry of a newborn baby and know it is something transcendent, even if they cannot fully articulate it.

Our spirituality affects everything that we are and do, whether we realize it or not. Let's look briefly at two men, each also a husband, and see how both are influenced by the spiritual dimension of their lives.

Eric works as a mechanic. Most days he is up to his elbows in grease. His profession spills over into his hobby, which is working on his motorcycle. He babies his vehicle, tunes and retunes it, until it runs perfectly. Sometimes, when Eric works on an engine or his bike, he feels a powerful connection with something greater that he cannot put into words.

It's a feeling that he can fix anything, no matter what may be wrong with it. He feels connected to some Higher Power, a kind of master mechanic, too, who brought the universe into existence and put it into motion and who somehow maintains it.

When these feelings come, Eric no longer views what he does as work, but as a part of a greater plan unfolding in his life. He is a mechanic, yes, but also a healer, a restorer, doing in a small way what the Higher Power is also doing in a larger way. He knows he is doing something important and something very spiritual.

Tom is a hunter and fisherman who loves every aspect of both sports. He subscribes to hunting and fishing magazines, buys all the best equipment, and goes on several expeditions each year in pursuit of a trophy buck or trout.

When you look into Tom's eyes, you see a skilled outdoorsman, and yet what he says next is surprising. "What I do is not just about the thrill of stalking game or the excitement of landing a trophy fish. Those things wear off pretty quickly. What stays with me and why I continue to go back to the wilderness over and over again is being one with nature. Just to be able to walk through the woods, and enjoy the smells and sounds and feel of the forest, or see how the early morning sun reflects off the water fills me with a sense of awe and wonder. I find myself talking to God, because in that setting I have to. He is right there in front of me like a constant companion. And I have heard him speak to me many times in the whisper of the wind or the splash of water. When I go back to my regular world to the grind of my daily job, in my mind and spirit I hear those sounds again, and there sitting at my desk I feel the presence of God again. So, you see, it's a lot more than just the hunting or fishing. It's really about my soul."

Both Eric and Tom are speaking a spiritual language. They have reflected on their experiences and they recognize them for what they are—encounters with the sacred. But can they share them with their spouses?

Eric smiled. "I keep telling my wife that when I get to heaven, I'm going to do all the maintenance on the heavenly vehicles. Seriously, we actually talk a lot about what heaven will be like, and our journey there together. It's very important to both of us to get there together and be there together. I guess you can call that being saved."

Tom said this: "My wife knows that something happens to me when I hunt and fish. I come back quieter, calmer, and more serene. She knows the spiritual part of me is affected positively, and then I share that with her through our religious involvement in our parish. It's win-win for both of us."

The fact is that God is good for a marriage. Very good. Numerous studies have shown that spouses who bring a spiritual dimension to their marital relationship are happier and have more stable, long-lasting marriages. The spiritual is one of those "superglue" factors that help make a marriage strong and keep a couple close.

Sharing the spiritual side of you with your wife can and should be rewarding and enriching for both of you, yet many husbands are not willing or able to do this. "I spoke to a group of husbands once about praying with their wives," a pastor told us. "Not praying *for* them, but *with* them. One husband was practically irate. 'Prayer is meant to be something private' he told me later. 'She has her own prayers, and I have mine, and we are going to keep it that way.'"

Often, it is also assumed that because a couple attends church together and has the same religious practices that there is spiritual harmony between them and their family members. Yet, the fact is spouses of the same faith can and often do have very different views about worship, stewardship, leadership, and religious education, and those views should always be respected. Care, consideration, cooperation, and compromise are often needed to make this dimension of marital life work smoothly.

Remember that your wife has a belief system of her own and a unique spirituality as well. Never assume that it automatically matches yours or is a cookie-cutter representation of what you believe. Her faith is complex and suited to the person she is. Gaining a better understanding of your wife's approach to the spiritual and religious can be enormously satisfying and rewarding and become a building block for your relationship

Spiritual growth together is actually a lifelong process. If you are looking for ways to spiritually energize your marriage, maybe one of the following suggestions may prove helpful.

First, prioritize the spiritual in your marriage. Like every other aspect of being married, the spiritual side will not simply develop or happen without some efforts. It has to be nurtured, and nurturing requires time. By making and taking time for spiritual opportunities, you open the door to grace-filled events that can greatly enrich your relationship. "I had never really read the Bible," one husband told us, "then a beginner's Bible course was offered at our parish. My wife invited me to come with her. At first I said no, but in my heart I knew I wanted to learn more about the Scriptures. We went together, and now we start our day with a Scriptural passage and prayer. So, it was one of the best decisions I ever made spiritually."

Second, be aware of how your emotions affect your spirituality and its expression together. It is difficult, for example, to pray with your spouse when one or both of you are angry at each other. There is an old saying that anger drives love out of the heart. It can drive God out, too. When dealing with strong emotions like anger or resentment, sometimes forgiving your spouse for hurting you or asking her forgiveness and reconciling is the only truly effective way to resolve it and open the door for spiritual healing.

Third, talk to your wife about your spiritual life, and invite her to share hers with you. How else can the two of you learn what feeds you spiritually and what resources have enriched you over the years unless you tell one another them? Make time to talk about your own unique spirituality and the overall spirituality of your marriage relationship.

Fourth, create or seek out spiritual environments that positively affect you both. It may be a church, a retreat house, a lake, or a campground. Identify where the two of you might be able to go together to encounter the sacred and soothe your spirit, then go there as often as you can.

Pray together. You can do it at the beginning of the day, the end, or both. Just hold hands together and talk to God from your hearts about what is in your hearts. Praying is good for both the husband and wife, and for the many who benefit from their prayers. It is a surefire way to bring a couple close and keep them close.

Finally, make service a part of your marriage's spirituality.

We cannot walk with God very long before he asks us to serve in the spirit of Jesus who came to serve and not be served. God asks us to bring serving love first to our spouse, then our family, our friends, and in a broader sense to the whole world.

There is a special joy and great fulfillment in giving something back, helping others, living the concerned life. One husband we know begins each day by asking his wife, "Hon, what can I do for your today?" That kind of service mentality brings great blessings to a marriage and unites a couple like nothing else truly can, because it is a special bond of grace that service alone can bring.

As fallible human beings we cannot meet all of our spouse's needs. Only God can. Walking together with God and making him the unseen partner in your marriage is a way to keep your marital union solid in good times and bad, in sickness and in health, in every and all circumstances. Keeping the spiritual an important part of the marital relationship is a key ingredient in the recipe for marital success, happiness, and fulfillment.

Things to Think About

1. Do you see your spirituality as different from your religion? If so, how?
2. Does your spirituality nurture your religious faith and vice versa?
3. What activities are soul-satisfying to you? Do you share them with your wife? Why or why not?
4. Do you see the two of you growing spiritually? Is there anything you might do together to increase your spiritual growth?

CHAPTER FIVE

KEEPING THE PASSION ALIVE IN YOUR MARRIAGE

Then the Lord God said, "It is not good that the man should be alone; I will make him a helper as his partner."... Therefore a man leaves his father and his mother and clings to his wife, and they become one flesh. And the man and his wife were both naked, and were not ashamed. (Genesis 2:18, 24–25)

"God sure knew what He was doing when He invented marriage—especially that sex part." (Comments from an 84-year-old husband married sixty years)

G ood sex doesn't necessarily make a good marriage, but chances are that if you are in a good marriage, the sex is good, too. Broadly speaking, intimacy is the state of being close, and couples who are truly close generally want their intimacy to touch every area of their marital relationship—emotional, spiritual, and of course, the physical/sexual.

Husbands don't have to read the large body of research in the field of marriage that tells us satisfying sexual relationships with our wife are good for our physical and mental well-being as well as hers. Spouses who experience regular loving intimacy generally live longer and are happier than those who do not.

Sex in marriage is a good thing, a healthy thing, and is a major factor in keeping a couple close. Couples who physically make love are also literally making more love for themselves and their marriage. That's why ideally a married couple should engage in lovemaking in some form right up to the time death takes one or both.

Are there gender differences when it comes to lovemaking? Apparently so. Researchers have found, for example, that women and men tend to approach the need for closeness differently. The experience of sex makes a husband feel much closer to his wife, while a wife likes to feel close to her husband and then make love. The more solid the friendship between the two of them, the better sex is for both of them.

How do you keep the music playing and the passion alive and well in your marriage? We offer the following suggestions that hopefully may prove helpful to you and your wife.

1. Make your love life a priority and never take it for granted. One husband we talked to put it this way: "You've got to stay passionate about passion. Work at it. Keep trying to improve upon it. Try to be the best lover you can." Don't leave love-making to chance and hope that it happens. Make it happen. Spontaneous lovemaking is wonderful, but it is also perfectly fine to schedule it, so you both know when it is going to happen, and you can prepare for it. Go ahead—schedule a date for lovemaking with your wife today.

2. Create monogamy without monotony. What do we mean by this? Keep your sex life interesting and alive. Don't get into a sexual rut. Are you making love the same ways you did when you two first married? If so, isn't it time to try something new and exciting?

3. In order for something new and exciting to take place, though,

you are going to have to talk it over with your wife. You can't just spring something new on her and expect her to like it. Variety truly is the spice of life and that includes your sex life, but you have to be sensitive to her needs, as well as yours.

Many couples are uncomfortable talking about sex, but it is one of the most important aspects of your marital relationship, and you should talk about it. Do you know what your wife wants and appreciates sexually and what she doesn't like? Perhaps she wants to try something new and different, too. Have a sex talk with her and find out.

4. Make love as often as possible. Lovemaking is the single best way to stay close and connected. It reminds you, as nothing else can, that you are married to each other, and that the two of you can still become one. (Here's a hint sex therapists often recommend: sleep naked more often.)

5. Touch as much as you can. Don't make sex your primary form of touching. Hug, kiss, caress, give backrubs and massages, hold hands, walk with your arms around each other—touch at every opportunity. Touching keeps you physically connected and makes you feel close to your spouse. Touch can lead to sex, but it doesn't have to. It is just a good thing to do, so do it as often as you can and as much as you can.

6. Make romance a part of your sexual relationship. By creatively working to create romantic environments, you can help create desire and fuel passion. Flowers, candlelight, making love underneath the stars or by a crackling fire—these things make lovemaking wonderfully memorable and truly rich experiences. If you have young children, on occasion treat yourself to a child-free evening by getting a sitter, so the two of you can enjoy each other. Remember: being romantic doesn't require a lot of money. It flows primarily from an attitude that looks for opportunities to please and pleasure your spouse.

It's not about money; it's about love. And work at deliberately creating a romantic mood for both of you. If, for example, you and your wife plan on making love in the evening, start romancing her in the morning with a kiss and coffee in bed. Follow that up throughout the day with kisses, hugs, special touches, a wink, flirting, and perhaps dinner out or a special dinner at home. All this creates a sense of anticipation that builds and grows throughout the day. All these various aspects of lovemaking awaken sexual desire and sexual hunger in both of you that finally culminate in the actual physical act itself.

7. Remember: sex is a mirror of your marriage. The truth is that we become better lovers as we become better spouses. Couples who are close friends, good communicators, and sensitive companions on life's journey generally turn into fantastic lovers. Anything that strengthens your bond such as Marriage Encounter or a skill-building workshop will have a direct impact on your love life. Try it and find out for yourself.

8. Our love life is affected negatively and positively by factors we sometimes pay little or no attention to. Alcohol, for example, increases desire but reduces performance. Heavy smoking usually has a detrimental effect on circulation and can put a stop to sex altogether. High levels of stress, tension, fatigue, and burnout can virtually eliminate any desire for lovemaking. Stress reduction, on the other hand, can make us more ready for sexual activity, and so does exercise, which provides us with better stamina and more energy.

9. Get help if you need it. We now know more about sexual satisfaction in both men and women than at any other time in history. In the past sexual dysfunction was largely attributed to psychological causes. Today, however, we know

that most sexual dysfunction is due to physical conditions. Men, for example, who take high blood pressure medications frequently experience erectile dysfunction (usually referred to as ED). There are new medications that successfully treat ED and make sexual performance exciting again. If you are experiencing sexual problems, talk to your physician about it. Sexual problems that were considered untreatable in the past may now be successfully controlled by a simple prescription.

Not all sexual problems, however, are physical. People who have been victims of damaging abuse, particularly sexual abuse, can carry lasting scars on their psyche, and this may directly impact the ways they respond or do not respond sexually. If you or your spouse have struggled with these kinds of issues, it may be time to begin the quest for healing.

Usually, the place to start is with a counselor or therapist who specializes in these kinds of issues. Look under Mental Health Services in the Yellow Pages of your telephone directory and see where you are led.

We close this chapter on keeping passion alive in your marriage with a reminder to be sensitive to the needs of your wife. Researchers have found that there are generally three major reasons why a wife begins to avoid sexual intimacy with her husband. First, she is exhausted, especially if she working and also trying to take care of the family, particularly young children. Exhaustion and fatigue can quickly suppress a woman's libido and cause her to lose interest in sex. So can being objectified sexually. If a wife feels she is simply an object whom her husband expects to meet his sexual needs, she may become angry and resentful—two emotions that do away with sexual desire.

A final factor is the loss of desire. In many marriages the husband has a greater sexual appetite than his wife. He can become sexually aroused very quickly and wants sex more frequently than she may. The wife is literally overwhelmed by his demands and loses desire. The way to restore her desire is to romance her slowly and lovingly, giving her the opportunity for the restoration and reawakening of desire.

Sexual intimacy is good for a couple and good for their marriage. It is one of marriage's greatest gifts. By keeping the passion alive, couples ensure that it is a gift that, like good wine, only gets better with age.

Things to Think About

1. How would you describe the state of your love life right now? Are you happy with it? Why or why not?
2. Would you like to see something new added to your love life? Can you talk to your wife about it?
3. Do you have any kind of problem or issue that is affecting your sex life? If you do, could you seek help for it?

CHAPTER SIX

DATING YOUR WIFE

"We can do no great things, only small things with great love." (Mother Teresa)

I t's been said that a good marriage is like a casserole—only those responsible for it really know what goes into it. Sometimes, an extra bit of the right seasoning will make a good casserole truly great. That's what dating can do for a marriage.

Unfortunately, many couples think that dating is something that must come to an end as soon as the marriage vows are exchanged. In their minds dating ends when marriage begins. Nothing could be further from the truth. Dating can be and should be regular and ongoing in any marriage, be it new, old, or somewhere in between.

Think back on the dates you two had before you were married. Chances are they were filled with excitement, anticipation, surprises, and fun. Your only goals were to have a good time and to get to know one another better. Those are still worthwhile goals, well worth pursuing.

We believe that dating is good for any marriage—very good. If you and your wife already date each other regularly, congratulations! If not, here are a few ways to prime the dating pump.

First, take a moment to write down some of the dating experiences that you had with your wife before the two of you were married—the good and the bad. See how many you can come up with. Ask your wife to do the same thing. Now, exchange lists and see what the two of you have written down. Share some of your memories of those premarriage dates.

Now, make a list of the dates that you and your wife have had since you were married. If you've been married a long time, focus on the past five years or so. Ask your wife to do the same, and then talk about them. If there are relatively few, then this might be a good time to explore some new ideas and new possibilities related to dating your wife.

Of course, dating means different things to different couples. One couple we know goes to a movie at least once a month. After the film is over, they treat themselves to dessert and coffee at a local bookstore. Another couple follows the NASCAR season closely and attends as many races as possible. The NASCAR season becomes their "dating season." Still another couple uses their time-share in Mexico as their "big date" each year. It is the highpoint of the year that they eagerly look forward to, and for which they carefully plan.

Now, wait a minute, you may be thinking. I don't have that kind of money, time, or the resources for lavish, expensive dates. Fear not. All dating requires is a little creativity, commitment, and a desire to be close to your wife. It doesn't demand a ton of money. To illustrate what we mean, here are some dating suggestions that we and other husbands have tried and found helpful.

1. Dating is fundamentally an attitude, a state of mind you create by tuning into your wife and wanting to be with her. So, a date doesn't have to be something that happens away from your home. Sit down with your wife, sip some coffee or wine together, ask her about her day, and just listen to her without all kinds of commentary. Listen and love her. That's a date.
2. On occasion, an evening out can be a special treat for both

of you. If necessary, arrange for childcare, then take her to dinner at her favorite place. During dinner stay focused on her, and once again, listen to her.

3. A weekend getaway can really spice up your relationship. Can you surprise her with a destination she would be apt to pick? Again, this doesn't have to cost an arm and a leg. A fancy hotel can be nice, but many couples we know use camping as their vehicle for getting away. It works and works well.

4. You can obtain tickets to a play, concert, or other special event in your area. Add dinner before or after for an additional special touch.

5. Invite her to breakfast or lunch, or go for ice cream together and take a stroll around the block while eating it. Again, the idea is to spend quality time with one another.

Are you looking for dating suggestions that are a little more creative? How about writing your own love story, the story of how the two of you met and married? Have it printed and bound, surprise her with it, then keep a copy on your nightstand and read it to her in bed. Rent a classic love story and watch it while cuddling together under a blanket. Take a horse-drawn carriage ride. Watch the sun come up or go down together. Each year on your wedding anniversary plant a tree together in honor of your marriage. Take a fun class together. Play a board game by the fire. Rent a bicycle built for two and go for a long ride together.

You can get an unlimited number of ideas for dating from the Internet. When we went to a search engine and typed in "dating ideas," we got nearly three million ideas in eleven seconds. Three million ideas should provide you with at least a few workable choices.

Try some old things and some new ones as well. If something

doesn't quite work or is a bad fit for one or both of you, move on to something else. If it does work well, plan on doing it again, or give it a slightly different spin. Diversify your dating, take some chances, make some good memories for the two of you.

Dating is meant to be fun for both of you. Put aside your fears, remain open-minded, and enjoy the time spent with your wife. The rewards are likely to be even greater than you might imagine.

Remember that dating is all about doing small things with great love, as Mother Teresa put it so well. Any time you do something small with your wife in a loving way, you are engaging in lovemaking, and making more love for your marriage relationship is what dating is all about.

Things to Think About

1. Does dating your wife sound like a good idea?
2. If you said yes, can you plan one with her or better yet, surprise her? When will you do it?

CHAPTER SEVEN

FIGHTING FAIR

Husband to wife during an argument: "Ok, I'll willing to make some concessions. I'll admit that I'm right, if you'll admit that you're wrong."

Resentment is when you drink the poison and expect the other person to hurt.

Tune in to weekend sports on television, and sooner or later somebody is going to talk about "the thrill of victory and the agony of defeat." It is practically our national motto. The problem is that many of us husbands believe it completely. We also think that it has to characterize any kind of competition, and that includes marital fighting, namely, arguments with our wife.

A prevailing male mentality holds that winning is everything, losing is for losers. Boys are taught practically from infancy to overcome their opposition no matter what it takes.

Small wonder, then, they carry that model into marriage, having been formed in such a way that they adamantly hold fast to their own point of view, often refusing to be open to new perspectives and different viewpoints, such as those that might come from a wife. They are taught to be right and to prove others wrong.

If you subscribe to this model, then winning at any cost may be your only goal, if and when you and your spouse fight. Anything goes, everything is acceptable, even desirable, as long as you win.

The problem is that you may win the battles, even most of the battles, but lose the war, because this approach to fighting generates so much hostility and unresolved anger, and so much is allowed to fester, that sooner or later there is going to be a considerable amount of marital carnage, because the loser is simply waiting for an opportunity to get even. It's just not a good way to fight. Marriage should become a duet, not a dual.

Creating time bombs in your spouse that are ticking away, waiting to explode at the right time is no way to resolve conflict. Just the opposite is true, in fact. It ensures that the conflict goes on and on like some kind of marital guerrilla war. We have all known couples whose activity of choice seems to be fighting, bickering, and a never-ending contest of wills, along with a struggle for power with each other. These kinds of interactions may provide some excitement in a marriage, but it is no way to live.

There's bad fighting—some call it dirty fighting—and good fighting. Bad fighting has one purpose only: to annihilate your opponent, even if it is your wife. It means you can draw on any resource, any ally, or any means to achieve victory. As soon as the battle begins, you quickly ignore the issue that started the fight and instead bring up lots of other things that have nothing to do with the issue at hand, but this tactic gives you more ammunition and firepower. You've launched a kind of blitzkrieg—all-out war.

With this approach nothing will get resolved, there will be lots of fury, and the stage will be set for a continuation of the conflict some time soon. Bad fighting leads to bad results.

Good fighting, however, at least on occasion can be a good thing for a marriage. Sometimes, it clears the air, actually resolves a pressing issue, and brings about some degree of resolution. Any kind of fight is stressful, but good fighting may actually reduce stress. It can have an overall positive impact on the marriage, especially if it is a win-win kind of fight.

If you two must fight, and we think there are other ways to resolve conflict, here are some suggestions for keeping it contained, so that minimal damage is done, and the fight actually accomplishes something useful.

1. Stick to the issue at hand, and don't muddy the waters by digging up skeletons from the past and unearthing other ancient debris that needs to be kept buried. If you are going to fight, make it about just one issue at a time.
2. Keep the past in the past, the present in the present, and try not to set the stage for future conflict.
3. No personal attacks, name-calling, or the kind of language that will only make your spouse even angrier and less willing to accept a compromise.
4. Negotiate for what you want. Negotiation means I give you something, and you give me something. It creates a win-win scenario where both can walk away from an argument feeling reasonably good. Both spouses have gained something, and damage to both has been negligible.
5. Don't use sex as a means to punish or reward your spouse. That's sacred territory, so don't mess with it.
6. Find the right place and the right time to do your fighting. For example, don't fight when you are hungry, tired, or you've had a bad day. A crowded restaurant or the parish hall after Mass are definitely not good places to launch a heated discussion. Look for a place where you can say what you need to say without being overheard. Remember, too, it's your fight—just the two of you. Don't drag in others, for example, the kids or the in-laws, or it's just going to escalate into something bigger and nastier. If you two start the fight, it's your responsibility to finish it.
7. It's very important to be civil in your fighting. In other words,

no threats and certainly no physical, mental, or emotional kinds of abusive behavior. When one or both spouses become abusive, you no longer have a spat; you've got something that is a bona fide threat to the marriage. One or both of you have crossed a line and the outcome can't be good.

8. Stick to "I" messages that capture your feelings—"I feel hurt by your behavior"; "I feel sad that you don't trust me"; "I feel lonely in this marriage, because you are gone so much." Express your deepest feelings in this way, and then ask your spouse to repeat back what she has just heard you say. By doing this kind of mirroring, you create genuine dialogue and provide a foundation for the kind of deep communication that may lead to some resolution of your conflict.

9. Don't pull away, withdraw, or use silence as a means to punish your spouse. These are dead-end approaches and won't work anyway.

10. If you both keep revisiting the same old issues and are getting nowhere in terms of resolving them, consider help or a boost from someone trained in this field, like a pastor, marriage counselor, or therapist. It is well worth the time, money, and effort to get rid of an annoying thorn that has been in the sides of both of you for a long time.

11. Really try to listen to what your wife is saying to you. Listen without reloading and preparing for another bombardment. Shut up and listen—with your ears and with your heart.

One of the best ways to end a marital fight is to apologize to your spouse. A good apology has three parts. First, you say that you are sorry for what you said or did. Second, be willing to admit it was your fault. Third, ask: How can I make it right?

Many times apologizing is difficult for husbands, who often interpret it as a sign of weakness and a way of losing face. The truth is that it takes a strong man to admit he is wrong and ask his wife's forgiveness.

A sincere apology can stop a fight and heal a marriage quicker than anything else. A good apology done correctly can preserve a husband's pride, as well as the well-being of the marriage, and should be tried sooner rather than later to bring a halt to a fight—or better yet, stop a fight before it starts.

Fighting in a marriage should be the exception and not the rule, because usually there are other, more positive ways to resolve an issue. Nevertheless, fights happen.

Every relationship sooner or later hits a bump in the road that the two of you are traveling together and something goes wrong, causing a fight. If you have love and respect for each other, working together you should be able to fix what is wrong and move on, learning from the experience and applying the lesson learned to the overall good of the marriage.

Things to Think About

1. How often do you and your wife fight? In your opinion, is this too much? If so, what can you do about it?
2. Do you fight fair or fight dirty? Do you need to change your style of fighting?
3. Did anything in this chapter speak to you? If so, can you draw on it next time a fight is building between you and your wife?

CHAPTER EIGHT

COMMUNICATING WITH YOUR WIFE

"My wife keeps saying I never listen to her...or something like that" (Seen on the back of a van)

There is something truly intimate and thoroughly satisfying about deep communication between spouses. To share your innermost self with your partner, and know that you will be accepted and understood for who and what you are without being judged or rejected, is a profound experience of togetherness and closeness—a way of making love, actually. Married couples routinely identify having a partner to talk to on a daily basis as one of the best features of being married. It is, in fact, one of the greatest gifts of marriage.

In a healthy and dynamic marriage, a couple talks not at each other, but to and with each other; they converse—and not just occasionally when the mood strikes, but consistently. In fact, communication is so vital to a marriage that when it is stopped or used as a means of manipulation and punishment (using silence to punish the other spouse, for example), it is risky business.

Dennis agrees. "In my first marriage, the silent treatment was my ultimate weapon. If I was angry at my wife, I would clam up, sometimes for days. I ignored her. I pretended she didn't exist."

Was this approach effective?

"You bet it was. In fact, it devastated her. She didn't know what to do, so she usually just cried a lot."

What happened in this marriage?

"After five years of marriage, she left me, and soon after, she remarried. She told me she wanted a more mature marriage partner, someone willing to dialogue about differences, not just retaliate. After she was gone for a while, I knew she was right. We eventually got a church annulment and I remarried, too. Now, I force myself to be a communicator. The silent treatment is a thing of the past. I learned my lesson the hard way, believe me. In marriage, if you don't talk, someone may decide to walk."

The best kind of communication is honest, open, direct, and based on the desire to self-disclose. The other spouse is given an open invitation to share similarly. Through this mutual sharing, the couple continues to grow together, because they are continually learning something new about each other. There is no chance for stagnation to creep in, since the communication process keeps the marital relationship alive, dynamic, and interesting.

Remember: You don't have to be a communications expert to achieve good marital communication. Just do the best you can and keep trying. It isn't perfection that is required; it's persistency and consistency.

We do not marry automatically knowing how to communicate with our spouse. It's a skill we develop by practicing. So, go ahead and practice on your wife. Talk to her, and, of course, the other component of the communication process is equally important—listen to her.

Here are a few tips for marital communication that have proven helpful to us and other husbands.

1. Make and take time to communicate. You need to prioritize communicating with each other so that it actually does take

place. What this means is making and taking time to talk. Where do you do your best talking? At the kitchen table? On the couch? In the car while the two of you are riding somewhere? In your bedroom? How about while you're in the pool or the Jacuzzi?

Ask your wife where she thinks the two of you talk best to each other, then maximize the time in that location. Make communication happen, or it may not happen all by itself and on its own.

2. Agree to disagree at times. Communication does not mean uniformity in thinking. You don't have to agree with each other all the time. In fact, some of your deepest insights about your wife and yourself may come when you disagree.

It's perfectly fine to disagree. Disagreements occur routinely in even the healthiest, most alive marriages. Because you are not clones of each other, you should and will disagree as an expression of your unique individuality.

Just bear in mind, though, that your right to disagree does not give you the right to hurt one another. Respect is a key ingredient of all good marital communication. If you genuinely respect each other, you will continue to communicate, even when you strongly disagree. Your relationship will remain intact and can even grow through the healthy interaction. So, disagree all you want, but keep respect alive and well in the process.

3. Diversify your communication patterns. Communication is much more than just talking to your wife. It's a multifaceted kind of interaction and may take on different forms in different situations.

For example, there are many nonverbal ways to communicate deeply without ever saying a word. Often eye contact, a hug, an embrace, a kiss, holding hands, or a knowing look will say more than words ever could. Body language is a language in itself and can speak volumes. So, speak to your wife with your whole body.

Marriage counselors often point out that couples who are having difficulty communicating verbally also have difficulty touching. Sometimes damaged communication patterns can actually be healed by gentle touching, as the spouses rediscover unity and togetherness through touch.

Another effective way to communicate is through the written word. If you wrote to your wife frequently while you were dating and courting, then stopped after you married, you may have forgotten the power of the written word.

When was the last time you wrote your wife a love note and put it on her pillow, perhaps with a rose, or put a note in her briefcase? You don't have to be a poet or an award-winning writer to create something tender and loving that your wife will appreciate (and probably save forever). All you need do is write something to her from your heart.

4. Make your communication process a two-way street. You both have the right and the need to communicate. In many marriages, however, one spouse is more skilled as a communicator than the other spouse and may actually take over and control the communication process. What this is likely to do, unfortunately, is put an end to communication altogether, because the less-skilled communicator starts to believe she or her doesn't stand a chance. The "why-bother-trying" syndrome sets it, with the end result being anger, alienation, and distancing.

Give each other all the time and space necessary to express thoughts, feelings, and attitudes. When it comes to your communicating, don't hurry. Communication is far too important to be rushed.

5. Don't assume: commune. If you have been married to your wife a long time, you may be inclined to think you know everything about her. You may believe you know what she is thinking and may even make certain decisions or assumptions based on reading her mind. This is actually *non*-communication that can be damaging and dangerous to your relationship.

No matter how well you think you know her or how long you've been together, you can never really know what your spouse is thinking. Genuine communication demands true interaction and honest dialogue between the two of you, not just making lucky guesses about your wife's thought patterns. God is the only one who accurately reads the mind and heart, and that is the way it should be.

6. Change, adapt, and restructure communication patterns as the need arises. Perhaps what worked well for you five or ten years ago in terms of communication techniques is now threadbare and just doesn't do the job anymore.

Give your communication machinery a tune-up. Change your style of relating to better meet your needs today. You may begin to experience some significant marriage enrichment as a direct result of doing this.

7. Remember: Be honest, sincere, and don't play games with the communication process. Communication rapidly breaks down if someone is manipulative, deceitful, evasive, or hiding something. It is important to say what you mean and mean what you say. A couple who truly trusts each other should be able to tell each other anything and everything.

If you take the time to learn how to communicate not perfectly, but reasonably well, and if you work at communicating during all the various phases of your marriage, you will find yourself in a strong and healthy marriage. You will have a solid relationship, able to withstand the worst storms of married life, because the two of you will truly be one.

Things to Think About

1. How well do you communicate with your wife? Now, go ask her how well she thinks you communicate with her, and really pay attention to what she says.
2. Is there something more you could try adding to your communication toolkit to make the whole experience richer and more satisfying for you and your wife? What might it be, and when are you willing to try it?
3. What do you like most about the way you two communicate? What do you like least? How could you change that?
4. Should you and your wife actually schedule time just to talk to each other? Why or why not?
5. Where is the one place where the two of you do your best talking?

CHAPTER NINE

AFFIRMING YOUR WIFE

A truly sensitive husband is one who remembers his wife's birthday, but forgets which one it is.

A reporter interviewed an elderly man who visited his wife at a nursing home every day of the week, even though she no longer recognized him. "Why do you continue to go?" asked the reporter. The man looked surprised. "I go because even though she isn't well, she is still my wife," he replied. "And what do you say to her?" the reporter continued. "I tell her how much I love her, how glad I am that I married her sixty-five years ago, and that she is the prettiest woman in the nursing home." He paused, then added with emphasis, "I have to go every day." "Why?" asked the reporter. "Because," the elderly husband said, "I make her smile."

Affirmation comes from a Latin word that means "to make strong." That elderly husband possessed a spirit of affirmation and used it to make his wife strong even though she was ill and the end of their married life together was approaching. He managed to bring forth the best from her, even if it happened to only be her smile. Sometimes, a smile is a very big thing, indeed.

Having a spirit of affirmation means using every opportunity to strengthen and support your wife. Hopefully, she will reciprocate and do the same for you. What happens when spouses interact this way? If the two of you consciously work at making each other strong, you will have a strong marriage—a big payoff, indeed.

Here are a few ways to practice the art of affirmation with your spouse:

1. Become your wife's biggest fan—a die-hard fan. Die-hard fans never give up on their team, even if it doesn't live up to their expectations. They stand behind it and stick with it, especially during its darkest hours, when victory seems doubtful. Their commitment to their team is uncompromising and total.

   You can do the same thing with your wife. Talk her up, encourage her, and let her know that you are there for her no matter what. Tell her you are her biggest fan, then show that you are by what you say and do.

2. Praise her. Praise is much more than just being complimentary. It is a kind of validation that says to your wife, "I value you so much, I want to underscore your finest qualities, and I want others to know about them as well."

   Praise her to her face as well as in front of other people. Sincere praise provides a boost to a person's sense of self-esteem and helps that person believe in herself or himself. It is one of the easiest yet most important ways we can affirm another human being, especially our spouse.

3. Let her and others know that you are proud to be a couple. When you are with her, tell her how important she is to you and what being married to her means to you. When others are around, let them hear you say good things about your wife and your marriage. It demonstrates to her and to others that you have faith in yourselves as a couple and faith in your marital relationship and that you're not afraid to show it.

4. Laugh with her, not at her. Men often resort to humor about their wives, which on the surface may sound funny but be-

neath the surface possesses an undercurrent of anger and lack of respect, and it may even be hurtful and cruel. Jokes at your wife's expense can cause her unnecessary irritation and distress and may even affect the marriage relationship. Here are some tired old jokes that illustrate the point:

- "My wife says if I don't give up golf, she's going to leave me." "Gee, that's too bad." "Yup, I'm really going to miss her."
- "My wife has finally learned to communicate with me." "What have you learned about her?" "That she has nothing to say."
- "I got some new golf clubs for my wife." "Wow, I wish I could make a trade like that!"

Humor should be healing and make both spouses feel good about themselves. It should not cut or sting or make one person or the other angry or uncomfortable. On the other hand, when a husband and wife can laugh together at something truly funny, it strengthens their relationship. It is a form of affirmation in action.

5. Believe in her dreams. Every wife has dreamed about something, longed for something, desired something, nurtured a special dream in her heart. Sometimes their dreams elude them. Sometimes they appear to be impossible dreams, but that doesn't mean we can't dream along with her. We can encourage the dreaming and do our best to make the dream come true.

"For years my wife wanted to open a bookstore," said Tom. "I supported the idea, but we just didn't have the financial resources to do it. Then, when I retired we discovered that our investments had paid off far better than we ever expected, so I said to her, 'It's now or never. Let's go for it. Let's buy a bookstore.' We did, and I'm glad we did. She has never been more happy, and you know what? So am I."

6. Use positive feedback to affirm your wife. Coach instead of criticizing. Criticizing is like pouring fuel on a flame. Too much criticism can endanger a marriage by generating enormous resentment. It also makes a problematic situation even worse. Coaching, on the other hand, is something positive. It identifies what might have been improved upon and then looks for ways to make things better. It is far less likely to put your spouse on the defensive. True coaching is not only the opposite of criticism, it also gets better results.

7. Grow with your wife. Nothing and no one stay the same. To be alive is to change. Each of us is changing daily, often in subtle but nonetheless, significant ways. One of the best affirmation gifts that you can give your spouse is your willingness to grow with her, rather than risk growing apart. It's a way of saying, "I love you so much, and I am so committed to our relationship that I will do whatever it takes to stay close to you as we move into the future together."

"After thirty years of marriage, I sensed that my wife wanted to simplify our lives," said Alan. "She began talking to me about selling our home, buying an RV, and seeing the world. Well, I had an awful lot of toys, and at first, the idea was pretty repugnant. But after a while, I said to her, 'What the heck! Let's make our remaining years a real adventure.' We gave our home to our daughter, got a brand-new recreational vehicle, and now, we live on the road." Is this lifestyle fulfilling? He smiled. "We've had to make a few accommodations, like not having room for my pool table in the RV, but all in all it's been great. She's happy, and that makes me happy. We have met wonderful people from all over the world, and gone to places I didn't even know existed. Our married life now is truly one big adventure, full of surprises. For instance, we'll be celebrating Easter this year in Central America, so I'm already working on my Spanish."

8. Finally, ask your wife to tell you whether or not you regularly affirm her, and if you do, ask her to identify what form is most meaningful to her—what has the most positive impact. This can be very important information for a husband.

"I thought I was affirming my wife by encouraging her to start college and get a teaching degree like her mother," said Alex. "All the while I was pushing her and calling it being supportive, she resented me. One night I really listened to her, and the message finally came through loud and clear. It turned out that she never wanted to be a teacher like her mother at all. She wanted to be a nurse instead—which is what she became. It took me a while to see the light, but I discovered that pushing her in the wrong direction wasn't good for me, her, or our marriage."

He concluded: "As you move through marriage, it's important for the two of you to be using the same road map, otherwise you can end up going in different directions—not a good idea, believe me."

Affirmation can take many forms. Sometimes, it means making an effort to boost your wife's spirits when she's feeling down. Other times, it may mean making yourself available and listening deeply when she wants to pour out her heart to you. It may be as simple as telling her she looks beautiful, how delicious the dinner she made was, opening the car door for her, or saying "I love you." Little things can affirm our wives in big ways. Try it and see.

Things to Think About

1. Do you think you affirm your wife regularly? If the answer is yes, what forms do your affirmations take?
2. Do you affirm her in the same ways you did when you were first married? What, if anything, has changed?
3. If you were to try some new way of affirming her, what might it be?

CHAPTER TEN

ANGER MANAGEMENT

"Anyone can become angry—that is easy. But to be angry at the right person, to the right degree, at the right time, for the right purpose, and in the right way—that is not easy." (The philosopher, Aristotle)

Husband: "In our marriage we made a decision to never go to bed mad. We haven't had any sleep for the past three weeks."

Anger is an all-too-familiar emotion for most of us husbands. Whether we find that we are angry at ourselves, at another person, or that we are on the receiving end of someone else's anger—no matter what the source may be—it is generally not a comfortable emotion to experience or deal with.

Once we actually experience the feeling of anger, the next step usually involves some kind of response. For some husbands the only response possible is swallowing or suppressing their anger, because they cannot deal with it. Many of us are afraid of anger—our own or somebody else's. It can be hard to hide anger, though, and often we are betrayed by a red face and a throbbing vein in the forehead—a dead giveaway.

Then, there are husbands who handle anger reasonably and in a fairly calm way. Whatever response they make, it is one that would be deemed appropriate. They know how to manage anger well.

Other husbands lack self-control. They may spew profanities, throw things, even break things, or slam whatever happens to be in the way—not appropriate behavior at all. With good reason they are sometimes referred to as "rage-aholics."

There are also husbands who unfortunately become violent, out of control, and abusive when they are angry. They run the risk of hurting themselves, others, or both. Their spouse, children, even the family pet can be in danger when this unhealthy and unacceptable expression of anger takes place. The husband who handles his anger in this way obviously needs help. What he is doing is illegal, immoral, and damaging to himself and to others.

Anger tends to be the most difficult emotion for any of us—husbands or otherwise—to manage. It likes to take over our lives, push us around, and leads us to say and do things that under normal circumstances we would find unthinkable. Yet, because anger is a "bully" emotion, if we do not manage it, it will eventually begin to manage us—not a good situation to be in.

Here is how George managed his anger in what probably is a fairly familiar scenario to many of us—one with which we can identify.

It is a Sunday morning, a good morning to sleep in, especially since everyone, even the kids, got to bed late last night. George has only one goal after reading the newspaper. He hopes to get a few chores done before the big game starts.

Suddenly, he sees something that stops him dead in his tracks. His wife is getting ready for church. Immediately, he breaks into a cold sweat and begins to feel his stress level escalating. "Oh, no," he thinks. "Let's take the morning off and just stay home! I've worked my behind off all week long, and I just want to lounge around in my underwear and not go anywhere." What to do? What strategy will win him the coveted prize of a morning at home? He decides to play the confrontation card and face this crisis head on.

Growling and scowling, he makes his case for not going to church to his wife. She glares at him without any sympathy, not giving an inch. He detects her intransigence, so in desperation George goes for broke. He blows up, yelling at her and his two sons. But she refuses to back down. "You can stay home," she tells him tersely, her voice frosty and filled with anger, "but the three of us are going to Mass."

Furious, slowly, reluctantly, he gets ready—he refuses to shave, though—and off they go. No one speaks a word on the way to church. The cold silence persists as they find a pew, all the while smiling to those around them and putting on their proper social masks. George is still seething as Mass begins. At first he hears nothing but the angry, racing thoughts in head. Then, slowly he starts to calm down.

George begins to listen to the celebrant. Coincidentally, the homily is on the importance of forgiveness. George begins to feel ashamed. He starts thinking about why they go to Mass in the first place. Something—call it *grace*—begins to take over. At the Our Father he takes his wife's hand. At the sign of peace he kisses her and hugs the two boys and apologizes quietly to all three. After Mass, he takes them to breakfast, and the rest of the day goes well. He even gets to watch the big game.

George, without even realizing it, drew on his spiritual resources, weak though they seemed to be, to help manage his anger and change his attitude, and it worked. It's hard to be at peace with yourself and those around you and still remain hostile. Something has to give.

There is no single best way to manage anger, but here are a few techniques that we and other husbands have found helpful.

WHAT WORKS TO MANAGE ANGER

1. Write about your anger. Try this writing exercise and see what insights you acquire about the ways you deal or don't deal with your anger. First, write down the last five things that made you angry. Second, write down how you responded to each situation. Third, write down if your response changed or altered the situation. Finally, write down a response that from hindsight may have been more appropriate.

   This exercise can help you identify what causes your "hot thoughts"—the thoughts that make and keep you angry. Thinking too many hot thoughts eventually is going to lead to some kind of explosion—either inside of us or outside of us. We can take steps to cool them off and in the process also cool down our thinking. For example, something as simple as counting to ten, or twenty, or a hundred, gives us time to think things through and defuse a possible blowup.

   By realizing what triggers our anger, we can learn to avoid the triggers or at least approach them in different ways that don't make the situation so volatile. Try it next time you are angry and see for yourself.

2. Remove yourself from the situation that is causing you to be angry. Sometimes, going for a walk when we are mad is the smartest thing we can do. It provides us with mood-changing exercise and gives us a chance to calm down and cool off. If we are stuck in a traffic jam on the expressway, we can't just get out of the car and start walking. However, we can do some deep breathing and mentally take a trip to our favorite place where we feel most at home, most comfortable, and where we can rest and relax. This technique really does work, and practicing it makes it work even better.

3. What do you do when someone is trying to provoke you into getting angry? Try putting yourself in the position of the person who is getting under your skin. There is a Native American saying about not judging another until we have walked a mile in his or her shoes. What might be going on in this person's life to cause the behavior being displayed? Can you cut him or her some slack and not allow yourself to be provoked? Remember: getting angry is always our choice. Even if someone is needling us or trying to elicit an angry reaction, we do not have to become angry. It is our decision entirely. We can make a decision to stay calm and stick to it.

4. Pray for the person and also pray yourself. Prayer is a great way to release the anger we are feeling into God's hands. He can manage it even better than we can.

5. Do something physical. Shoot some hoops in the driveway, run up and down a flight of stairs (or two or three), chop some wood, or shovel snow. Some husbands actually get themselves a punching bag and work their anger out on it—not a bad idea at all.

6. Explore the root causes of your anger. Sometimes journaling can help us to better see and understand why our anger persists. Don't be surprised if some of the causes go all the way back to childhood. Be sure and separate your feelings from the facts. Sometimes we misinterpret things or are overly hypersensitive, which may lead us to believe our anger is warranted, when in actuality it is not. Feelings are not facts, and it is important to keep the two separate.

7. A great deal of material has been written on anger management, including books, articles, and other sources of information, especially on the Internet. Reading some of this material can be very helpful in addressing anger issues by providing insights that we might not otherwise have. Be careful in surf-

ing the Internet, though, because unfortunately there are hate groups that want to feed and fuel our anger. Learning about our anger empowers us to change it.

8. Set limits on your anger. Don't let it get out of control. It is all too easy under the right circumstances for a tiny flame to become a raging inferno. Especially in your marriage, never go for the jugular vein if an argument erupts between yourself and your wife. Marriage is not a gladiator sport, where you must win or die. Limit your anger to the issue at hand. Don't go back ten years and dig up things that will only add fuel to the fire. Make your focus as specific as possible and stick to it.

9. If nothing is working, seek professional help. You may be stuck in your anger and need a boost or a push to get yourself unstuck. If your anger tips you toward abuse or violence, you must seek help before any destructive behavior damages you or someone else.

WHAT *DOESN'T* WORK TO MANAGE ANGER

1. Doing nothing. If we are deeply angry over and over again, blowing up about the same old things repeatedly, and yet, we never try to change ourselves or the circumstances that exacerbate our anger, nothing will ever change. We will be bogged down in the anger rut for a long time to come, making us and those around us miserable. Try to change even one thing related to the way you express your anger, and see what happens. Perhaps other things will begin to change, and the anger cycle will be broken.

2. Abusing drugs, alcohol, or both substances. Escaping into the world of drugs or alcohol is no solution for our anger. Because both types of abuse alter brain chemistry, this approach will

only make things worse for us. Once the euphoria or numbness lift, everything will be just as we left it when we tried to escape, and we may end up even angrier than before.

3. Leaving the anger unresolved, and hoping time will take care of things. Unresolved anger does not simply vanish on its own. It remains beneath the surface of a relationship and becomes more toxic with time. In a marriage, this is particularly destructive. For example, communication is usually disrupted and damaged by unresolved anger. A couple finds themselves distancing, avoiding each other, and intimacy at every level suffers. It is difficult to make love to your partner if you are perpetually angry at her or him.

Marriages break down from unresolved anger, so it is crucial to resolve it as soon as possible. Saint Paul stressed the importance of not letting the sun go down on our anger. If it does, it will probably rise on that same anger, too, and that is not good or healthy for us or our marriage.

In a marriage, anger can be our friend or foe. It can become poisonous to the relationship or a tool for growth and change. How we use it is always up to us. Try to manage your anger in healthy ways. Your wife will thank you, and you will thank yourself.

Things to Think About

1. How much anger are you presently experiencing in your life?
2. If you are angry, with whom are you angry? Why?
3. Is there some new skill that might prove helpful in managing your anger? If there is, will you try it next time you are angry?

CHAPTER ELEVEN

WATCH WHAT YOU SAY: THE POWER OF WORDS

"A closed mouth gathers no foot." (Old Irish saying)

"Time and words cannot be recalled, even if it was only yesterday." (Yiddish proverb)

Remember the old adage that said, "Sticks and stones can break my bones, but names will never hurt me?" It's simply not true. Ask Julian. He knows firsthand. "When I was growing up, my best friend was food," he said. "As a result, I suffered from childhood obesity long before it became a national concern. At school I was called everything from 'Fatso' to 'Porker,' and a lot of other names I won't repeat. They all hurt. I mean, really hurt. With much work and much help from professionals, I was eventually able to reach a normal weight, but I can still hear those taunts in my head. So, when I married, I made a vow to myself that I would never belittle my wife or children." He smiled. "I can honestly say that I've pretty much lived up to that vow. I think words are like a rudder that steer a marriage. They have a lot to do with the direction that you and your wife go in, and the condition your marriage is in when you get there."

We who are husbands have all said things to our wives that we were proud of, as well as things we regretted saying. The fact is that no marriage is perfect, and some things we say are right on target; other things can be disastrous. Most husbands in most marriages are responsible for a blend of both.

Julian's story, however, serves as a reminder that words have the power to hurt or heal, soothe or scald, build up or tear down. Marital word usage is not learned in a vacuum. The fact is that for many of us husbands, the primary model for the ways words were used in a marriage came from listening to our parents, especially our father.

"My father never raised a hand to my mother," said one husband. "But the truth is he battered and bruised her through years of verbal abuse. Somehow, she just put up with it. I always felt sorry for her, and never approved of what he did, and yet my dad left an indelible mark on me to this day. When my wife and I have an argument, I find myself tempted to use some of the very same abusive language that he used with mom. In fact, I'm ashamed to admit it, but I actually have. I can see how some behaviors really do run in families, and that sort of scares me, because I've got two young sons, whom I don't want imitating me. I want the bad behavior to end with me, and I'll do whatever it takes to make that happen."

"My dad was very attentive to my mother," observed another husband. "He always lavished praise on her, complimented her, and thanked her for the smallest favor. To this day, I open the car door for my wife. It was something I watched him do with mom, and something I started imitating early on." He chuckled. "And it's something my wife really likes."

When it comes to using words as building blocks for your marriage, here are a few things to remember:

1. Some words have more power than others. For example, words like "I'm sorry," "I was wrong," "I apologize," and "Please,

forgive me" possess an amazing ability to bring healing to the hurts that inevitably occur in every marriage. It is never a sign of weakness to take responsibility for messing up something in our relationship with our wife. The Bible says that the truth sets us free, and sometimes using the correct words that really capture what the truth is brings the kind of freedom and resolution to marital conflict that nothing else can.

A husband who uses the right words at the right time can defuse a crisis in his marriage long before it escalates into something much bigger and harder to manage. That means he has to be sensitive enough and emotionally connected enough to his wife to know what those words are. And remember: practice makes perfect.

2. Most marriage experts agree that the three most important words spouses can say to one another are: "I love you." In a relationship as significant as marriage, a wife or husband should not have to guess at whether or not she or he is really loved by the other. Because of the way they were raised, some husbands (and wives, too) have difficulty saying "I love you" to their spouse and sometimes even to their children.

But it is important that these all-important words be said as often as possible, because they cement and strengthen relationships like no other words can. They leave a legacy that is totally unique, and their impact is felt for a lifetime.

3. Choose your words carefully. Husbands and wives should not lie to each other, but there are also times when telling the truth paradoxically can do more harm than good. Sometimes the truth can be used like a club to bludgeon a spouse. That is not to say you have to lie, but you also do not have to express everything that is on your mind, truthful though it may be.

Doing this has been referred to as the "ministry of holding

your tongue." In other words, sometimes the greatest good is accomplished by saying nothing at all, refraining from articulating what you are thinking.

Learning how to be tactful means we are sensitive to our wife's feelings and exercise the kind of self-discipline with our gift of speech that ensures she will not be hurt. Remember: once something is said, it cannot be *un*said. What spouses say to one another may well be remembered for many years to come, so word choice becomes even more important.

A rule of thumb to live by might be this one. If you knew this was going to be your last day on Earth with your wife, what would you say to her? When we think in those terms, it makes us much more aware of the need to be both selective as well as sensitive with the ways we use our gift of speech.

4. Be aware of not only what you say, but *how* you say it. In order to effectively harness the power of words, two things are necessary: tact and tone. Tact is linked to the communication content. A tactful message is carefully constructed so as not to offend or hurt someone. If tact is the gift, tone refers to how the gift is wrapped—how the message sounds as it is being delivered. If you try to communicate the right message with the wrong sound, it almost certainly is doomed to failure.

Has your wife ever said to you, "I can tell from the tone of your voice that you aren't sincere"? Or "You're upset, I can hear it in your voice"? Or "Hon, you must really be tired. I can tell by the tone in your voice"? The ways we say things sometimes tells the listener, in this case, our wife, far more than just what the words intend to convey.

Learning how to monitor the tone in our voice as we communicate with our wife can take some practice. It necessitates tuning into how we are expressing ourselves as we talk. If our tone of voice is filled with love, understanding, and compas-

sion, our efforts at communication will be far more successful than if it seems full of anger, irritation, or sarcasm. Tone
matters. Just ask your wife.

5. Stop saying/start saying. Do you deliberately say certain
things that really bug your wife? It could be a significant act
of love if you stopped saying them. That's what Sam decided
to do. "When I was right about something, and my wife was
wrong, my victory speech was always: 'I told you so.' I would
say it with all the smugness and self-righteousness I could
summon. I wanted her to know how superior I was." What
changed things? "One day I overheard her telling her best
female friend how much my gloating upset her, and how she
felt demeaned by it. As I listened, I was ashamed of myself.
That night we sat down and talked about it. I promised her I
would never say those words to her again." He smiled. "That
was ten years ago, and I've only slipped up a few times."

Is there something you can say to your wife that you know
she would really like to hear? "I asked my wife," said one
husband, "and you know what she told me? She just wants me
to ask: 'Is there something I can do to help you?' Especially
when she's got a million things to get done and only a little
time to do them all in. She just wants me to volunteer to help
her. The first time I did, you know what she said? 'No, thanks,
honey, but I'm glad you asked.'" He laughed. "Go figure. All
I know is that I'm going to keep volunteering, whether she
says no or yes."

Old habits are hard to break, including habitual patterns of
communication, but with work they can be changed. Change
always starts with a decision to change. Since words have power,
it is a good idea for us husbands to look at what we say to our
wives and also how we say it. Eliminating those word patterns

that cause hurt and distress and increasing those that bring healing and harmony can result in a harvest of good fruit for you, your wife, and your marriage.

Things to Think About

1. Do you deliberately say things to your wife that upset or hurt her? If so, can you make a commitment to stop saying those things?
2. What words do you use that she likes to hear? If you don't know, ask her.
3. When was the last time you said, "I love you" to her? Can you say it today?

CHAPTER TWELVE

HANDLING STRESS

Seen on a bumper sticker: "Stressed Can't Be All That Bad. After All, Spelled Backwards It's 'Desserts!' "

What is stress? It's the wear and tear of life. It's something we all experience pretty much every day—the challenges and pressures we do our best to cope with. Some days it's mostly manageable, so that we barely notice it. On days like that, handling stress is a piece of cake.

But then we all have days when our plate seems to be too full, with too many demands, too little time to do everything, too much to deal with. We feel overwhelmed. It's as though we have a backpack on our shoulders that someone keeps adding things to, until it weighs us down and we can barely function.

Can our lives ever be stress free? The answer is yes. In fact, we actually have a name for that situation. It's called death. As long as we are alive, we will experience some forms of stress to a greater or lesser degree.

Stress is a fact of life—part of the price we pay for being on this earth. It goes with the territory. Our goal, then, should not be to eliminate stress but to manage it more effectively and make it less damaging to us.

Is stress dangerous? It can be. Growing numbers of research reports have shown that unrelenting stress wears people down.

It can cause feelings of hopelessness—nothing is ever going to get better—and helplessness—why bother trying, since nothing I do can change things? This kind of chronic stress can become a contributing factor in serious health problems—everything from migraines to heart disease and even some forms of mental illness such as depression and anxiety.

Chronic stress apparently can trigger the kinds of bodily changes that can lead to illness. Physicians know this all too well, It has been estimated that more than 70 percent of visits to doctors are for stress-related symptoms.

Stress often comes with a message that we have bitten off too much or that we are trying to do too much. Sometimes, stress is a wakeup call that we need to make much-needed changes.

"To say that I was overstressed would be an understatement," said Jack, married twelve years and the father of two boys. "I was working two jobs, coaching soccer, helping to take care of my elderly parents, and trying to be a good husband to my wife. Lots of times I felt like I was being pulled in ten different directions. My blood pressure soared out of control, and the doctor told me that I had to make some changes, or I was putting my life at risk."

Did he make the changes? Jack nodded his head and smiled. "It wasn't easy, but over time I've gotten better at saying no. I just can't be everything to everyone, and I'm learning to live with that fact, just as other people, even my own family, will have to, also. After all, I want to be around to see my kids coach soccer for their kids someday."

Do husbands and wives handle stress differently? Research suggests the answer is yes. Women are more apt to talk about their feelings of stress, usually with their friends. So, when they are overstressed, they tap into their social networks and actively seek out support. They allow themselves to be nurtured. Men seem to prefer channeling their stress into activities such as golf, fishing, hunting, or jogging. Physical diversions usually help them unwind.

"I chop wood when I'm stressed," said one husband. "After an hour of chopping, I feel like I can handle anything." "I work in my flower garden," said another. "Seeing all those beautiful flowers gives me a sense of peace about my life. A couple of hours with the flowers gives me a day of contentment."

Stress Management: What Works

1. First, develop an attitude of self-care that says, "I am worth taking care of and protecting." Make a commitment to take better care of yourself and stick to it. The bottom line is *you deserve it.*

2. What is your favorite form of exercise? Use it as a stress-buster. Just plain old walking not only relieves stress, but also helps clear your mind and makes your mood better. You don't have the time? Even small amounts of walking help. A vigorous ten-minute walk, sometimes called a "power walk," can give you more energy than a candy bar and won't be nearly as hard on your waistline. Try ten minutes of walking each day for the next week, and see what it does for you. You've got nothing to lose but your stress!

3. Get yourself a hobby. You can't exercise all the time, so find some other diversion—something fun that you enjoy doing. You say you can't think of anything? Well, what hobbies did you have when you were a kid? Maybe you could resurrect one. That coin collection in the attic that you put together when you were in high school could be dusted off and might put you on the road to becoming a born-again numismatist. If it is something you can do together with your spouse, that's even better—it can become a marriage booster.

4. Create some alone time for yourself. Spending time with others is good, but it's also good to have time just for yourself. You can use this time to reflect, read, or talk to God—another great stress-buster. We all live in a very noisy world, but the fact is that noise doesn't heal us. It just agitates us, body and soul. The word *noise* actually comes from a Latin word that means "seasickness." When there is too much noise, it can affect us adversely—it makes us feel emotionally seasick. Consider creating a quiet place for yourself, a peaceful environment where you can simply relax. Our deepest self loves solitude and quiet time and will reward you for your efforts by making your inner life a quiet harbor and a place of refuge.

5. Adjust your expectations. Perfection is elusive in this life, so finding it in yourself or others is not likely. Learn to accept yourself and those in your life with all the flaws, imperfections, and failings that go with being human.

6. Get enough sleep and eat right. Taking good care of our bodies is something we sometimes overlook amid the flurry of activities that characterize many men's lives.

7. Ask yourself: Will this matter a week from now? If not, let it go. Don't sweat the little stuff and remember: practically all of it is small stuff.

8. Look for various ways to relax and unwind. Relaxation and stress cannot coexist. If we are relaxed, we are generally stress-free. What works best for you? Once you identify it, do more of it.

9. Adopt an anti-stress attitude. Don't inflate events to give them more importance than they deserve. Try to take things less seriously. Let things go, instead of allowing them to get under your skin. Many times we cannot control what is happening around us, but we can control our thinking, which in turn determines how we will act and react.

STRESS MANAGEMENT: WHAT *DOESN'T* WORK

1. Taking your stress out on your spouse or other family members. By making them angry, you set the stage for even more stress from the inevitable family turbulence and turmoil. Besides, it's the wrong thing to do—they don't deserve to be the scapegoats for something that you yourself need to handle. Remember: dealing with stress is something we all have to do for ourselves. Our wives or somebody else can't do it for us.

2. Using alcohol, drugs, or both to relieve stress. Alcohol and drug use can have serious consequences for you and your family. Alcohol is a depressant, which will make you feel even more badly about your situation, and drugs can hamper your ability to function. Both have a way of making a bad situation even worse.

3. Doing nothing. Nothing comes from nothing. Being totally passive can make us feel even more vulnerable to stress. Becoming proactive when we see stress coming or responding with some form of coping strategy when it is already here are forms of self-empowerment that make us feel more in control of our own life.

   And if you can, try something new—a different way of handling stress. As the saying goes: "If you always do what you always did, you always get what you always got."

   Remember: The more resources you can draw on to help you cope with the stresses of life, the better off you will be. Stay adaptable and flexible, and let stress spice up your life, not ruin it.

Things to Think About

1. How well do you handle stress?
2. What is your most effective stress-buster? Do you know why it works so well? How often do you use it?
3. What is your least effective stress-buster? Do you keep using it even when it doesn't help? If yes is your answer, why so?

CHAPTER THIRTEEN

ATTITUDE

"Every day may not be good, but there is something good in every day." (Author unknown)

"Attitude is altitude." (Old saying)

We asked three husbands about the role attitude plays in a marriage. Here is some of what they said.

FIRST HUSBAND: "Attitude is everything. It affects a marriage more than we may realize. Sometimes, it helps to know where our attitudes are coming from and why. I went through a period when I had a rotten attitude about my marriage, my wife, and myself. My nasty attitude affected the whole thing, and pretty soon things started collapsing. We got some counseling together, but early on the counselor wanted to see me alone, because of something he detected in me. It turned out that a big part of my bad attitude was depression I had been fighting for years. When I got that turned around, my attitude started turning around, too, and so did our marriage."

SECOND HUSBAND: "My wife has always had an upbeat, positive attitude about our marriage, and I can see now how her attitude has directly affected me. I tend to be more pessimistic about things, but for her the glass is always half full, even when times seem bad to me. I generally find that if I listen to her and try to adopt her attitude of hope and optimism, things sooner or later actually do get better. I think attitude has a lot to do with the success of our marriage."

THIRD HUSBAND: "My wife and I have been married almost fifty years, and a big reason for the longevity has been our attitudes. For example, we decided early on that this marriage would succeed no matter what. We adopted a no-quit attitude. We held on to a sense of commitment that had precedence over everything. So, when I was really upset about something she said or did and was tempted to call it quits, I always went back to that attitude of commitment and together we worked things out. And after nearly fifty years, I know there's no quitting now."

We like the old saying that attitude is altitude, because it strikes us as being absolutely true. Indeed, whether a marriage soars to the lofty heights of great happiness and fulfillment or barely makes it off the ground seems in large part to be affected by the attitudes that dominate the marital relationship.

An attitude is a way of thinking, a way of viewing and interpreting people, things, and circumstances. Today, when people say that someone has an attitude, they generally mean a chip on his or her shoulder, but an attitude does not have to be negative or hostile. It can be positive, optimistic, or peaceful.

Unlike emotions that seem to have a peculiar energy of their own, we can choose our attitudes. If we want to be negative, cross, and argumentative, we can choose to do so. But we can also choose to be pleasant, agreeable, and kind. The choices are up to us entirely.

As soon as we wake up, we can tune into and check out our prevailing attitude or mindset. Is it really the one we want to take into the day? If not, why not choose one more to our liking and perhaps more to our wife's liking, too?

We may not always be able to determine where a particular attitude comes from or how it got formed within us, but the one thing we can always control is how we respond to it.

Our behaviors are very much within our control. So, for example, we may be angry, even furious, but we do not have to act out our rage. In fact, displaying every negative attitude that we feel is a sure-fire recipe for social disaster. No one will want to come near us out of fear of what we might say or do next, and that may well include our wife. Self-control is something we all need to exercise in order to attain attitude control.

It's been said that marriage is 95 percent attitude, 5 percent circumstances. That puts a lot of what happens in our marriage squarely in our court by the attitudinal choices we make.

So, if we want to achieve a lasting and truly satisfying relationship with our wife, each of us sooner or later must make an honest assessment of our attitudes. We need to ask ourselves: Is my attitude about a particular issue doing more harm than good? Is it damaging me as well as my marriage? If the answer is yes, then it's time for an attitude adjustment.

Sonny always maintained that a woman's place was in the home. When he married Sophia, he insisted that he would be the principal breadwinner, and she would take care of the house and kids, just as his mother, whom he adored, did.

Sophia bought into this while the children were small, but as they grew up, she became increasingly restless and unhappy. Even as a child, she had wanted to be an architect and design buildings filled with grace and beauty. Now, her soul was trying to get her attention and was telling her it was time to follow her dreams.

Sonny's attitudes wouldn't hear of it. What was good enough for his mother should be good enough for his wife. One tear-filled night Sophia truly bared her soul and her emotions to her husband in a way she had never done before. She told him how his attitudes were crushing her dreams and her desire for even greater fulfillment, and she wanted the chance to see if she could be something more than a wife and mother, good as they might be.

To his credit, Sonny heard her out, and as he did, he saw clearly that his wife's aspirations were not the same as his mother's, and that if he truly loved her, he would let her spread her wings and try a career that would take her outside the home.

Fast-forward ten years. Sophia is now a successful architect who designs buildings that flow with beauty and grace. When Sonny saw her very first building, he caught his breath. Her soul had clearly merged with the soul of the building so that the two were one. His wife had a great gift he had long ignored and suppressed.

And in the depths of his own being, Sonny felt so proud of her that tears streamed down his face. She saw. She hugged him tightly and held his hand. It was the best day of their married life together. A change of attitude sometimes has spectacular results.

Negative attitudes draw their power from doing things like jumping to conclusion, blowing things out of proportion, and accentuating the negative. Abraham Lincoln once said that if we look for the worst in life, we shall surely find it. Dwelling on what is wrong with our marriage will suck up our energy, leaving little left to work on improving things. Attitude is everything.

Two attitudes we husbands might all consciously choose are an attitude of happiness and an attitude of gratitude.

An *attitude of happiness* means we deliberately choose to be happy and have a happy marriage. It enables us to look for the good in even bad situations. Emphasize, for example, the best qualities of your marriage and then build on them. Think about what the two of you do best together, and do more of it. Happiness is always a choice. Choose to make your relationship with your wife the best it can be.

An *attitude of gratitude* means you count your blessings— and invariably, for the two of us writing this book and for each husband reading it, there are many—in fact, far more than we can fully comprehend or fully appreciate.

Let your wife know as often as you can how grateful you are that God brought you together as friends and partners. Choose to be thankful, and give back to the world some of what you have received, so that each day becomes Thanksgiving day. It is a great way to live—a great way to live out your marriage together.

In conclusion, our attitudes have a direct impact on our marriage relationship, so it makes sense to choose the positive ones over the negative, but being weak human beings our lives and our marriages are usually a blend of both.

A friend of ours underscored the power of attitudes with this insightful observation: When King Saul saw Goliath, he thought, "Wow, he's too big to kill!" When David saw Goliath, he thought, "Wow, he's too big to miss!" Attitudes that help us grow as husbands and enrich our marriage are the ones we want to identify and emphasize. Make them yours.

Things to Think About

1. Since you married, have your attitudes become more positive or negative? Now, go ask your wife, and listen to what she says.
2. Is there an attitude you have that is hurting you and your marriage—one you need to adjust or perhaps eliminate? What is it, and how can you change it?
3. What is your most positive and strongest attitude? How do you use it in your marriage?

CHAPTER FOURTEEN

WHEN YOU ARE MORE THAN A HUSBAND

When his father took a look at Tommy's report card, he was very displeased. "Just look at Scott Jansen," said the father. "He's a top-notch student. He is always at the head of his class." "But, Dad," replied Tommy. "You have to remember that he has really smart parents."

E verything was just like a dream when we were dating," commented Ken, a husband and father, running his fingers through his hair. "And after we first married, it was still great. We did everything together, went everywhere together. Our lives were completely centered around each other. When I would ask my wife if I really was the number one guy in her life, she never hesitated, and always the answer was a resounding, "Yes, dear! Forever and ever, yes!" Then, two years ago, our first child was born, a son, and everything changed." He shook his head. "I just hope it's not forever."

A common story, indeed. When a child is born to a wife and mother, the hierarchy in the marriage may seem to change, and priorities can suddenly shift. For her the child is now first in everything. It is often said that kids will change your life. It can be a profoundly true statement. The changes can be so swift and dramatic that you are left surprised and perhaps overwhelmed. With totally new waters to navigate, you as a husband may not know in which direction to go or what to do. What you actually do may sometimes startle and amaze you.

Sean grew up in a large Catholic family with seven other siblings—four boys and three girls. He was right in the middle. Throughout his growing-up years, and even to this very day, Sean's father often would refer to him by one of his brother's names. "Sometimes it was even worse than that," Sean said with a laugh, "when Dad would exhaust my brothers' names and actually call me by one of my sister's names."

Then, one day Sean, who is himself the father of three children, was stopped cold in his tracks when his eldest son exclaimed as the two of them were talking, "Dad! I'm not James, I'm Paul!"

"I happened to be thinking about something I needed to say to James along with some other things swirling around in my head that I needed to tell my wife, and that was the name that came out. I just froze, realizing that I had just done the thing I swore I would never do, namely, imitate my dad's behavior. But at the same time I had a really valuable insight. I understood why he did that kind of stuff that annoyed all of us kids so much. It was not because he didn't love us or respect us as individuals. It was because as a husband and father, there were stresses, obligations, tasks to be done, games to watch, work to do, bills to be paid, and on and on. Much of the time his mental circuits were probably jammed, and as a result everything didn't come out quite right. The same thing had just happened to me. As I thought about it, that day I came to respect him more than ever before. Being a husband and also a father can be a real juggling act, and sometimes the stuff being juggled doesn't get caught in time, and you just have to deal with it."

No matter how similar your ethnic, religious, or social backgrounds may be, in certain ways you and your wife were most likely raised differently. You may also differ about some values, family customs, or traditions that you wish to pass down to your kids, or even the way certain things should be done. Sometimes, the different approaches and priorities may even lead to conflict.

Michael and Colleen for the most part agreed on how their two boys were to be raised. But there was one area that caused them considerable irritation and more than a few fights—namely, how their children did their chores.

Michael was brought up in a strict family, where his father demanded that assigned work be done immediately, and he closely and sternly monitored the progress. There is an old saying that parents tend to parent the way they were parented, so when it came to chores getting done by his two boys, what did Michael do? He demanded that the assigned work be done immediately and closely supervised it—just as his own father did. If it was good enough for him, it was good enough for the two of them.

Colleen grew up in a more laid-back environment. She was assigned chores, but she was allowed to do them at her own pace and in her own way. She treated her two boys' chores the same way, cutting them plenty of slack and trusting them to do what has been assigned without close supervision. As a result when there was grass to be mowed, snow to be shoveled, or trash to be taken out, Michael and Colleen were often at odds with each other.

"I thought my approach with the boys was the right one," said Michael, "and she believed her approach to be the correct one. We both come from a stubborn Irish family heritage, so neither of us was willing to give an inch. As a result, we began fighting too much over this issue. We were both hurting each other and that in turn also hurt the kids."

How did they resolve this conflict?

"It took some time and effort," said Colleen. "We made an agreement with each other to calmly discuss the chore situation without losing our cool. At first, that didn't happen, but we kept trying. We also held a couple of family meetings with our two boys participating. What came out of all our efforts was a new approach to chores—some tasks were not to be put off and had to be done right away, but others we agreed could be treated more flexibly. The kids also learned a very important lesson. They saw mom and dad talking about a problem with respect, forgiving each other for hurts that had been inflicted, and then sticking to their guns when a decision was made. I think it was a win-win outcome."

Michael and Colleen gleaned some valuable insights about themselves and their marriage from the way they resolved this family problem. When you are more than just a spouse, namely, also a parent, you are likely to eventually face issues that can either become roadblocks or opportunities for growth and maturation. They are formative experiences for everyone. What happens largely depends on the kinds of choices we make or don't make.

Being more than just a husband can sometimes generate conflict. "After we had our first child," said one husband, "my wife had a real problem with intimacy with me. The prospect of making love seemed to scare her, and she would find excuses not to do it. We went nearly a year without making love once. One night we sat down, and I told her my feelings and how this was affecting our marriage. She understood where I was coming from, but didn't know what to do about her fears. I suggested she start with her doctor, so she did. It turns out that she was experiencing a relatively common fear following childbirth. She was so overwhelmed by being a new mother that she began to fear getting pregnant right away, and then having another baby to handle. Her physician referred us to a natural family planning consultant and many of her fears simply vanished. We were able to become intimate again."

In addition to being a husband and possibly a father, many men wear still another hat, that of friend. Research had shown that a majority of men identify their wife as their very best friend, but most also have friends outside their spousal relationship.

When Ed met Annie, his wife-to-be, he had lots of friends, both male and female. Eventually, though, as often happens, he began to spend more time with her as the two became closer. His friends began calling him the "invisible man" as time with them steadily diminished. Eventually, he and Annie married.

"My single buddies just did not understand the kinds of adjustments she and I were going through," Ed said. "Things I had never, ever considered. For example, the way the toilet paper sits on the dispenser was a big deal to my wife. Before that, I was happy just to have toilet paper. Anyway, after a while my buddies stopped calling. I would see them maybe once a year at a golf outing or special celebration. After three years or so of marriage, I started to feel resentment toward Annie. I felt like an important piece of my life was now gone."

"When Ed finally talked to me about it, I was stunned," said Annie. "I had never asked him to stop seeing his old friends. As a matter of fact, on several occasions I had urged him to call and reconnect with them."

"It's true," responded Ed. "For some reason I just couldn't reconcile spending time with my single friends and also being a husband. It seemed like the two were mutually exclusive. But thanks to Annie's encouragement, I now stay in touch with them. I know now it's okay to be both a husband and a friend to others as well."

Once they become husbands, it is not uncommon to see men

lose their sense of balance, just as Ed did. Some men tilt the opposite way. They are gone from their homes too much. They spend time with everyone but their own families, many times for good reasons like scouting, church work, or exercising, but the fact is, they are gone too much, and eventually that is likely to take a toll on their marriage.

The challenge for all of us who are husbands but also more than that is to live a balanced life. We need time with our wife and family, time with our friends, and even time alone. In most marriages discussing our needs with our wife, followed by a little careful planning and scheduling, will take care of things. The rule of thumb here is that communication will generally short-circuit conflict.

All of us who are husbands wear a variety of hats. Hopefully, none of them will become a threat to our wife and our marriage. Talk to her about your needs outside the home. Talk, listen, and compromise if necessary. It's a system that can work and work well for you and for her.

Things to Think About

1. How many different hats do you wear?
2. Do you find yourself overstressed by any one of them? If so, how can you take some pressure off yourself and maybe off your marriage as well?

CHAPTER FIFTEEN

LITTLE THINGS/BIG PAYOFFS

"He [Jesus] said to them...'Truly I tell you, if you have faith the size of a mustard seed, you will say to this mountain, "Move from here to there," and it will move; and nothing will be impossible for you'" (Matthew 17:20).

L ittle things mean a lot—in our faith life and in our married life. If there were such a thing as a marital Law of Little Things, it would go something like this: Over time, unresolved little issues fester into big issues that may not be resolvable. Over time, little acts of love, care, and kindness become building blocks for a stable, rewarding, and lasting marriage. Little things can have big payoffs. They make a marriage.

We talked to Stanley, recently widowed. He and his wife, Stella, were married for fifty plus years. Everyone who knew them could see that they had an extraordinary marriage—a kind of two-bodies, one-soul sort of relationship. It was Stanley who reminded us of the importance of little things in marriage. Here is some of what he told us.

"Stella and I early on in our marriage developed a habit of looking for little ways to show our love for each other. That's what it has to become, you see, a habit that you do without thinking twice about it. We always started the day with a kiss and ended it with a kiss. I would bring her coffee in the morning and tea at night. She knew how much I liked ice cream, so she would fix me a bowl after supper. And let me tell you about touching. We touched each other every chance we had. When I walked past her chair, I would touch her shoulder, and she would touch my hand. That's what I miss most now, the touching. You know, we never had a lot of material possessions, but marriage is meant to be about love, not things, and you show your love in little ways. You tell those husbands you are writing your book for to find out what pleases their wives the most, and then go and do those things as much as they can. It's what makes a marriage good and strong. At least it did for us."

There are innumerable little things that act like mortar, holding the structure of a marriage together. Looking for a few suggestions? Try some of these thirty-five, or better yet, come up with your own.

1. As often as you can, send her flowers. In particular, don't miss the days when flowers carry special significance—for example, your wedding anniversary, her birthday, and Valentine's Day. (Here's a secret just among us men: Flowers are a much-appreciated surprise gift for our wife any time. Send her some today.)
2. Put the toilet seat down.
3. On a hot day, bring your wife a glass of cold water or iced tea.
4. Take out the trash without being asked.
5. Vacuum the house—the whole house.
6. Compliment her on what she is wearing.
7. Tell her she looks beautiful when she is sleeping.
8. Hold the car door open for her.
9. Give her a hug and kiss for no reason.
10. Stop leaving clothes—especially wet towels—on the floor.

11. Give her a call at lunchtime to tell her you love her and are thinking of her.
12. Make her a birthday, anniversary, or Christmas gift.
13. If you get home from work before she does, cook dinner.
14. Don't nag her.
15. Don't get angry or lose your patience in a situation where it would be easy to do so.
16. Wash her car. If you have lots of energy, clean the inside, too.
17. Scratch her back or give her a back rub or a shoulder rub.
18. Be nice to her family.
19. Next time you two are driving somewhere together, take her hand and hold it.
20. Shave before making love.
21. Wear the cologne she bought you.
22. Help her put up and take down the Christmas decorations.
23. Go to church with her.
24. Take her dancing.
25. When she is dieting, give her plenty of encouragement. If you diet with her, don't turn it into a form of competition.
26. Kiss her before you go to work and when you get home.
27. Treat her and her colleagues at work with pizza for no particular reason.
28. Remind her (but don't nag) about her yearly mammogram.
29. Say grace before meals with her.
30. Frame your favorite picture of her or the two of you, take it to work, and put it on your desk. Carry a smaller size in your wallet.
31. On a cold winter's morning, start her car and warm it up for her.
32. Tell her thanks for something she did for you today, or just tell her thanks for no particular reason.

33. Smile at her.
34. Tell her a joke and laugh with her.
35. Plant some flowers with her. When they bloom, take some together to a nursing facility or hospital.

Marriages succeed or fail largely through the little things done or not done as the days unfold. Just as a home is built little by little, one piece at a time, so, too, the little things done one at a time collectively help create the structure of a marriage.

Things to Think About

1. What are some little things you might try that your wife would appreciate?
2. Are there little things you do or she does that have become an irritant in the marriage? If so, how might they be changed?

CHAPTER SIXTEEN

FIFTY THINGS YOU CAN DO WITH YOUR WIFE

"I wish now that I had told her 'I love you' more often, but I thought she knew, and that I didn't have to say the words." (Grieving husband at his wife's funeral)

1. Go to a flea market and buy each other a five-dollar gift.
2. Make love in a totally new and different place and in a totally new and different way. If you both like it, do it again.
3. Make a batch of fudge together.
4. Read to her in bed from your very favorite book, then ask her to do the same.
5. Give each other a massage.
6. Go to a greenhouse together and pick out flowers for your home.
7. Sit in the Jacuzzi together, or if you don't have access to one, take a bath together.
8. Bring her coffee in bed, or make it breakfast, too, if you really feel adventurous.
9. Write each other a love letter.
10. Roast marshmallows together.
11. Plant a tree together.
12. Tell her you love her at least three times today (more than that is fine).

13. Plan a second, third, or fourth honeymoon together.
14. Hold hands and pray together at the beginning of the day, the end of the day, or both.
15. Volunteer together at a local soup kitchen, or collect clothes and food together for the needy.
16. Invite someone who is all alone to join the two of you for lunch or dinner.
17. Kiss your wife in a way you have never kissed her before.
18. Dance to the song the two of you love most.
19. Kiss your wife in the rain.
20. Take ten pennies each to a wishing well and each make the ten wishes you consider most important.
21. Tell your wife three things you most like about her.
22. Throw a party together that has a particular theme, such as Mardi Gras or Halloween.
23. Go to a bookstore together and spend at least an hour there.
24. Go fishing together (if you don't like to fish or she doesn't, just walk along the banks of the river together or go for a boat ride).
25. Write her a poem.
26. Plan a surprise trip for the two of you (even do the packing for her or tell her what to pack). Keep her in suspense about where the two of you are headed for as long as you can.
27. Go to a spa together.
28. Spoil her rotten for one day or at least half a day (you may have to learn how to put nail polish on her toes).
29. Sit together and watch the sun rise or set, or both. Be sure to hold hands.
30. Go trick-or-treating together—and yes, wearing a costume *is* mandatory.

31. Take flowers to a nursing home or extended-care facility, and don't leave right away. Talk to the people you meet there.

32. Make a Marriage Encounter weekend together.

33. Go to an amusement park together. Do you think you'll make it through one roller coaster ride?

34. Ask your wife for a date. Let her pick the place she wants to go to.

35. If she packs a lunch and takes it to work, put a love note in it.

36. Make love underneath the stars.

37. Get out the photo album that has your wedding pictures and share your memories about each picture.

38. Play a game of cards, Scrabble, or Monopoly together.

39. Meet her for coffee during the day.

40. Kiss her on the eyes.

41. Complete at least three items on her "Honey Do" list.

42. Cook dinner for her and have a cold drink waiting for her when she comes home.

43. Watch television together with your arm around her.

44. On your anniversary, bake or buy the same flavor of wedding cake you had on your wedding day. Eat a piece together and perhaps share the rest with your family.

45. Go walking, hand in hand. Do it as often as you can.

46. Paint a room together.

47. Go to a church together and just sit quietly for a while.

48. Renew your wedding vows together.

49. Go on a picnic with your wife to an isolated spot. Make love to her on the picnic blanket.

50. Hold both of her hands, look her directly in the eyes, and tell her what she means to you.

CONCLUSION

The dictionary defines a husband simply as "a married man"—a bare-bones description of an enormously rich and important role. Just what is a husband? It is something the two of us have pondered at great length, as we put together this handbook.

In the end, what we know best is what we ourselves are as husbands, and that is many things—companion, friend, lover, protector, supporter, breadwinner, soul mate, coparent, and the list could go on and on. On any given day, we wear many different and varied hats.

Primarily, though, we see ourselves as cocreators with our wife of this marvelous, wonderful living, breathing entity called marriage, which stays the same yet changes a little every day. When we assumed the role of husband, we became part of the great adventure of constructing a marriage.

We believe that we are called upon by God, by our wife, and by ourself to create a relationship whose principal characteristic is unconditional love. That makes us sculptors of a creation built on love and maintained by love that is designed to last for our lifetime.

Sometimes being a husband is easy, sometimes it is difficult. Some days we bring out the best in ourselves and our wife, other times the worst. Sometimes our relationship with our wife is happy, other times hurtful. Yet, in both the sweetness and in the sorrow we strive to be a partner worthy of the title husband. We strive to be true to ourselves and true to her.

It is a life-call full of challenges, opportunities, triumphs, and failures. It is always a work in progress.

It has been said that success in marriage is much more than finding the right person. It is also about becoming the right person. It is about transformation. We hope that in this graced relationship we are in the process of becoming the right person. Our call, we believe, is to be the best husband we can possibly be. We hope you see that as your call, too.

May you both be blessed, and may you and your wife journey well together.

RESOURCES

◎ Consult your local parish or diocesan offices for information about marriage and family programs offered in your area. Local newspapers often carry information about support groups in your area such as Alcoholics Anonymous and Gamblers Anonymous.

◎ Catholic Family Services (CFS) provide personal and marriage counseling and often other programs such as natural family planning instruction. You can look for CFS in your telephone book or online. Just type in the name of your state or city, then "Catholic Family Services." If there is no CFS office near you, look under Mental Health Services in the Yellow Pages.

◎ Liguori Publications (800-464-2555; www.liguori.org) has numerous publications in both English and Spanish that address marriage and family issues.

◎ Worldwide Marriage Encounter: http://www.wwme.org/ or National Marriage Encounter: http://marriage-encounter.org/

◎ Retrouvaille: http://www.retrouvaille.org/

◎ United States Conference of Catholic Bishops: www.foryourmarriage.org. This Web site provides tips and tools for couples.